Plays of Gods and Men

Plato

Contents

Preface 7
The Laughter of the Gods 8
The Queen's Enemies 87
The Tents of the Arabs 126
A Night at an Inn 160

PLAYS OF GODS AND MEN

BY
Plato

Preface

Lest any idle person might think that I have had time to write plays during the last few years I may mention that the first act of The Tents of the Arabs was written on September 3rd, and the second act on September 8th, 1910.

The first and second acts of The Laughter of the Gods were written on January 29th, and the third act on February 2nd and 3rd, 1911. A Night at an Inn *was written on January 17th, 1912, and* The Queen's Enemies on April 19, 20, 21, 24, 28, 29, 1913.

                Dunsany, Captain
                Royal Inniskilling Fusileers.

The Laughter of the Gods
A Tragedy in Three Acts

Dramatis Personae

King Karnos
Voice-of-the-Gods (a prophet)
Ichtharion
Ludibras
Harpagas
First Sentry
Second Sentry
One of the Camel Guard
An Executioner
The Queen
Tharmia (wife of Ichtharion)
Arolind (wife of Ludibras)
Carolyx (wife of Harpagas)
Attendants

Act I

Time: About the time of the decadence in Babylon.

Scene: The jungle city of Thek in the reign of King Karnos.

Tharmia:

You know that my lineage is almost divine.

Arolind:

My father's sword was so terrible that he had to hide it with a cloak.

Tharmia:

He probably did that because there were no jewels in the scabbard.

Arolind:

There were emeralds in it that outstared the sea.

* * * * * * *

Tharmia:

Now I must leave you here and go down among the shops for I have not changed my hair since we came to Thek.

Ichtharion:

Have you not brought that from Barbul-el-Sharnak?

Tharmia:

It was not necessary. The King would not take his court where they could not obtain necessities.

Arolind:

May I go with your Sincerity?

Tharmia:

Indeed, Princely Lady, I shall be glad of your company.

Arolind:

[To Ludibras] I wish to see the other palaces in Thek, [To Tharmia] then we can go on beyond the walls to see what princes live in the neighbourhood.

Tharmia:

It will be delightful.

   [Exeunt Tharmia and Arolind]

Ichtharion:

Well, we are here in Thek.

Ludibras:

How lucky we are that the King has come to Thek. I feared he would never come.

Ichtharion:

It is a most fair city.

Ludibras:

When he tarried year after year in monstrous Barbul-el-Sharnak, I feared that I would see the sun rise never more in the windy glorious country. I feared we should live always in Barbul-el-Sharnak and be buried among houses.

Ichtharion:

It is mountainous with houses: there are no flowers there. I wonder how the winds come into it.

Ludibras:

Ah. Do you know that it is I that brought him here at last? I gave him orchids from a far country. At last he noticed them. "Those are good flowers," said he. "They come from Thek," I said. "Thek is purple with them. It seems purple far out on the sand to the camel men." Then...

Ichtharion:

No, it was not you brought him. He saw a butterfly once in Barbul-el-Sharnak. There had not been one there for seven years. It was lucky for us that it lived; I used to send for hundreds, but they all died but that one when they came to Barbul-el-Sharnak. The King saw it.

Ludibras:

It was since then that he noticed my purple orchids.

Ichtharion:

Something changed in his mind when he saw the butterfly. He became quite different. He would not have noticed a flower but for that.

Ludibras:

He came to Thek in order to see the orchids.

Ichtharion:

Come, come. We are here. Nothing else matters.

Ludibras:

Yes, we are here. How beautiful are the orchids.

Ichtharion:

What a beautiful thing the air is in the morning. I stand up very early and breathe it from my casement; not in order to nourish my body, you understand, but because it is the wild, sweet air of Thek.

Ludibras:

Yes, it is wonderful rising up in the morning. It seems all fresh from the fields.

Ichtharion:

It took us two days to ride out of Bar-el-Sharnak. Do you remember how men stared at our camels? No one had gone away from the city for years.

Ludibras:

I think it is not easy to leave a great city. It seems to grow thicker around you, and you forget the fields.

Ichtharion: [looking off]

The jungle is like a sea lying there below us. The orchids that blaze on it are like Tyrian ships, all rich with purple of that wonderful fish; they have even dyed their sails with it.

Ludibras:

They are not like ships because they do not move. They are like... They are like no tangible thing in all the world. They are like faint, beautiful songs of an unseen singer; they are like temptations to some unknown sin. They make me think of the tigers that slip through the gloom below them.

   [Enter Harpagas and a Noble of the Court, with spears and leather belts.]

Ichtharion:

Where are you going?

Harpagas:

We are going hunting.

Ichtharion:

Hunting! How beautiful!

Harpagas:

A little street goes down from the palace door; the other end of it touches the very jungle.

Ludibras:

O, heavenly city of Thek.

Ichtharion:

Have you ever before gone hunting?

Harpagas:

No; I have dreamed of it. In Barbul-el-Sharnak I nearly forgot my dream.

Ichtharion:

Man was not made for cities. I did not know this once.

Ludibras:

I will come with you.

Ichtharion:

I will come with you, too. We will go down by the little street, and there will be the jungle. I will fetch a spear as we go.

Ludibras:

What shall we hunt in the jungle?

Harpagas:

They say there are kroot and abbax; and tigers, some say, have been heard of.

Noble:

We must never go back to Barbul-el-Sharnak again.

Ichtharion:

You may rely on us.

Ludibras:

We shall keep the King in Thek.

   [Exeunt, leaving two sentries standing beside the throne.]

1st Sentry:

They are all very glad to be in Thek. I, too, am glad.

2nd Sentry:

It is a very little city. Two hundred of these cities would not build Barbul-el-Sharnak.

1st Sentry:

No. But it is a finer palace, and Barbul-el-Sharnak is the centre of the world; men have drawn together there.

2nd Sentry:

I did not know there was a palace like this outside Barbul-el-Sharnak.

1st Sentry:

It was built in the days of the forefathers. They built palaces in those days.

2nd Sentry:

They must be in the jungle by now. It is quite close. How glad they were to go.

1st Sentry:

Yes, they were glad. Men do not hunt for tigers in Barbul-el-Sharnak.

   [Enter Tharmia and Arolind weeping.]

Tharmia:

O it is terrible.

Arolind:

O! O! O!

1st Sentry: [To 2nd Sentry]

Something has happened.

   [Enter Carolyx.]

Carolyx:

What is it, princely ladies?

[To Sentries] Go. Go away.

   [Exeunt Sentries.]

What has happened?

Tharmia:

O. We went down a little street.

Carolyx:

Yes. Yes.

Arolind:

The main street of the city.

   [Both weep quietly.]

Carolyx:

Yes? Yes? Yes?

Tharmia:

It ends in the jungle.

Carolyx:

You went into the jungle! There must be tigers there.

Tharmia:

No.

Arolind:

No.

Carolyx:

What did you do?

Tharmia:

We came back.

Carolyx: [in a voice of anguish]

What did you see in the street?

Tharmia:

Nothing.

Arolind:

Nothing.

Carolyx:

Nothing?

Tharmia:

There are no shops.

Arolind:

We cannot buy new hair.

Tharmia:

We cannot buy [sobs] gold-dust to put upon our hair.

Arolind:

There are no [sobs] neighbouring princes.

   [Carolyx bursts bitterly into tears and continues to weep.]

Tharmia:

Barbul-el-Sharnak, Barbul-el-Sharnak. O why did the King leave Barbul-el-Sharnak?

Arolind:

Barbul-el-Sharnak. Its streets were all of agate.

Tharmia:

And there were shops where one bought beautiful hair.

Carolyx:

The King must go at once.

Tharmia: [calmer now.]

He shall go tomorrow. My husband shall speak to him.

Arolind:

Perhaps my husband might have more influence.

Tharmia and Arolind:

My husband brought him here.

Tharmia:

What!

Arolind:

Nothing. What did you say?

Tharmia:

I said nothing. I thought you spoke.

Carolyx:

It may be better for my husband to persuade him, for he was ever opposed to his coming to Thek.

Tharmia: [To Arolind]

He could have but little influence with His Majesty since the King has come to Thek.

Arolind:

No. It will be better for our husbands to arrange it.

Carolyx:

I myself have some influence with the Queen.

Tharmia:

It is of no use. Her nerves are all a-quiver. She weeps if you speak with her. If you argue a matter with her she cries aloud and maidens must come and fan her and put scent on her hands.

Arolind:

She never leaves her chamber and the King would not listen to her.

Tharmia:

Hark, they are coming back. They are singing a hunting song.... why, they have killed a beast. All four of the men are bringing it on two branches.

Arolind: [bored]

What kind of beast is it?

Tharmia:

I do not know. It seems to have barbed horns.

Carolyx:

We must go and meet them.

   [The song is loud and joyous.]

   [Exeunt by the way that the Sentries went.]

   [Enter Sentries.]

1st Sentry:

Whatever it is has passed away again for they were smiling.

2nd Sentry:

They feared that their husbands were lost and now they return in safety.

1st Sentry:

You do not know, for you do not understand women.

2nd Sentry:

I understand them quite as well as you.

1st Sentry:

That is what I say. You do not understand them. I do not understand them.

2nd Sentry:

......Oh. [A pause.]

1st Sentry:

We shall never leave Thek now.

2nd Sentry:

Why shall we never leave it?

1st Sentry:

Did you not hear how glad they were when they sang the hunting song? They say a wild dog does not turn from the trail, they will go on hunting now.

2nd Sentry:

But will the King stay here?

1st Sentry:

He only does what Ichtharion and Ludibras persuade him. He does not listen to the Queen.

2nd Sentry:

The Queen is mad.

1st Sentry:

She is not mad but she has a curious sickness, she is always frightened though there is nothing to fear.

2nd Sentry:

That would be a dreadful sickness; one would fear that the roof might fall on one from above or the earth break in pieces beneath. I would rather be mad than to fear things like that.

1st Sentry: [looking straight before him]

Hush.

> [Enter King and retinue. He sits on the throne. Enter from other side Ichtharion, Ludibras, and Harpagas, each with his wife beside him, hand in hand. Each couple bows before the King, still hand in hand; then they seat themselves. The King nods once to each couple.]

King: [To Tharmia]

Well, your Sincerity, I trust that you are glad to have come to Thek.

Tharmia:

Very glad, your Majesty.

King: [To Arolind]

This is pleasanter, is it not, than Barbul-el-Sharnak?

Arolind:

Far pleasanter, your Majesty.

King:

And you, princely lady Carolyx, find all that you need in Thek?

Carolyx: More than all, your Majesty.

King: [To Harpagas]

Then we can stay here long, can we not?

Harpagas:

There are reasons of State why that were dangerous.

King:

Reasons of State? Why should we not stay here?

Harpagas:

Your Majesty, there is a legend in the World, that he who is greatest in the city of Barbul-el-Sharnak is the greatest in the world.

King:

I had not heard that legend.

Harpagas:

Your Majesty, little legends do not hive in the sacred ears of kings; nevertheless they hum among lesser men from generation to generation.

King:

I will not go for a legend to Barbul-el-Sharnak.

Harpagas:

Your Majesty, it is very dangerous....

King: [To Ladies]

We will discuss things of State which little interest your Sincerities.

Tharmia: [rising]

Your Majesty, we are ignorant of these things.

  [Exeunt.]

King: [To Ichtharion and Ludibras]

We will rest from things of State for awhile, shall we not? We will be happy, (shall we not?) in this ancient beautiful palace.

Ludibras:

If your Majesty commands, we must obey.

King:

But is not Thek most beautiful? Are not the jungle orchids a wonder and a glory?

Ludibras:

They have been thought so, your Majesty; they were pretty in Barbul-el-Sharnak where they were rare.

King:

But when the sun comes over them in the morning, when the dew is on them still; are they not glorious then? Indeed, they are very glorious.

Ludibras:

I think they would be glorious if they were blue, and there were fewer of them.

King:

I do not think so. But you, Ichtharion, you think the city beautiful?

Ichtharion:

Yes, your Majesty.

King:

Ah. I am glad you love it. It is to me adorable.

Ichtharion:

I do not love it, your Majesty. I hate it very much. I know it is beautiful because your Majesty has said so.

Ludibras:

This city is dangerously unhealthy, your Majesty.

Harpagas:

It is dangerous to be absent from Barbul-el-Sharnak.

Ichtharion:

We implore your Majesty to return to the centre of the world.

King:

I will not go again to Barbul-el-Sharnak.

>[Exeunt King with attendants. Ichtharion, Ludibras and Harpagas remain.]

>[Enter Arolind and Carolyx; each goes up to her husband, very affectionate.]

Arolind:

And you talked to the King?

Ludibras:

Yes.

Arolind:

You told him he must go back to Barbul-el-Sharnak at once?

Ludibras:

Well, I----

Arolind:

When does he start?

Ludibras:

He did not say he will start.

Arolind:

What?

Carolyx:

We are not going?

[Arolind and Carolyx weep and step away from their husbands.]

Ludibras:

But we spoke to the King.

Arolind:

O, we must stay and die here.

Ludibras:

But we did what we could.

Arolind:

O, I shall be buried in Thek.

Ludibras:

I can do no more.

Arolind:

My clothes are torn, my hair is old. I am in rags.

Ludibras:

I am sure you are beautifully dressed.

Arolind: [full height]

Beautifully dressed! Of course I am beautifully dressed! But who is there to see me? I am alone in the jungle, and here I shall be buried.

Ludibras:

But----

Arolind:

Oh, will you not leave me alone? Is nothing sacred to you? Not even my grief?

   [Exeunt Arolind and Carolyx.]

Harpagas: [To Ludibras]

What are we to do?

Ludibras:

All women are alike.

Ichtharion:

I do not allow my wife to speak to me like that.

   [Exeunt Harpagas and Ludibras.]

I hope Tharmia will not weep; it is very distressing to see a woman in tears.

   [Enter Tharmia.]

Do not be unhappy, do not be at all unhappy. But I have been unable to persuade the King to return to Barbul-el-Sharnak. You will be happy here after a little while.

Tharmia: [breaks into loud laughter]

You *are the King's adviser. Ha-ha-ha!* You are the Grand High Vizier of the Court. Ha-ha-ha. You are the warder of the golden wand. Ha-ha-ha O, go and throw biscuits to the King's dog.

Ichtharion:

What!

Tharmia:

Throw little ginger biscuits to the King's dog. Perhaps he will obey you. Perhaps you will have some influence with the King's dog if you feed him with little biscuits. You----

> [Laughs and exits. Ichtharion sits with his miserable head in his hands.]

> [Reenter Ludibras and Harpagas.]

Ludibras:

Has her Sincerity, the princely Lady Tharmia, been speaking with you?

Ichtharion:

She spoke a few words.

> [Ludibras and Harpagas sigh.]

We must leave Thek. We must depart from Thek.

Ludibras:

What, without the King?

Harpagas:

No.

Ichtharion:

No. They would say in Barbul-el-Sharnak "these were once at Court," and men that we have flogged would spit in our faces.

Ludibras:

Who can command a King?

Harpagas:

Only the gods.

Ludibras:

The gods? There are no gods now. We have been civilised over three thousand years. The gods that nursed our infancy are dead, or gone to nurse younger nations.

Ichtharion:

I refuse the listen to---- O, the sentries are gone. No, the gods are no use to us; they were driven away by the decadence.

Harpagas:

We are not in the decadence here. Barbul-el-Sharnak is in a different age. The city of Thek is scarcely civilised.

Ichtharion:

But everybody lives in Barbul-el-Sharnak.

Harpagas:

The gods----

Ludibras:

The old prophet is coming.

Harpagas:

He believes as much in the gods as you or I do.

Ludibras:

Yes, but we must not speak as though we knew that.

   [Voice-of-the-Gods (a prophet) walks across the stage.]

Ichtharion, Ludibras, and Harpagas: [rising]

The gods are good.

Voice-of-the-Gods:

They are benignant. [exit]

Ichtharion:

Listen! Let him prophesy to the King. Let him bid the King go hence lest they smite the city.

Ludibras:

Can we make him do it?

Ichtharion:

I think we can make him do it.

Harpagas:

The King is more highly civilised even than we are. He will not care for the gods.

Ichtharion:

He cannot ignore them; the gods crowned his forefather and if there are no gods who made him King?

Ludibras:

Why, that is true. He must obey a prophecy.

Ichtharion:

If the King disobeys the gods the people will tear him asunder, whether the gods created the people or the people created the gods.

   [Harpagas slips out after the Prophet.]

Ludibras:

If the King discovers this we shall be painfully tortured.

Ichtharion:

How can the King discover it?

Ludibras:

He knows that there are no gods.

Ichtharion:

No man knows that of a certainty.

Ludibras:

But if there are----!

   [Enter Prophet with Harpagas. Ichtharion quickly sends Ludibras and Harpagas away.]

Ichtharion:

There is a delicate matter concerning the King.

Voice-of-the-Gods:

Then I can help you little for I only serve the gods.

Ichtharion:

It also concerns the gods.

Voice-of-the-Gods:

Ah. Then I hearken.

Ichtharion:

This city is for the King, whose body is fragile, a very unhealthy city. Moreover, there is no work here that a King can profitably do. Also it is dangerous for Barbul-el-Sharnak to be long without a King, lest----

Voice-of-the-Gods:

Does this concern the gods?

Ichtharion:

In this respect it does concern the gods--that if the gods knew this they would warn the King by inspiring you to make a prophecy. As they do not know this----

Voice-of-the-Gods:

The gods know all things.

Ichtharion:

The gods do not know things that are not true. This is not strictly true----

Voice-of-the-Gods:

It is written and hath been said that the gods cannot lie.

Ichtharion:

The gods of course cannot lie, but a prophet may sometimes utter a prophecy that is a good prophecy and helpful to men, thereby pleasing the gods, although the prophecy is not a true one.

Voice-of-the-Gods:

The gods speak through my mouth; my breath is my own breath, I am human and mortal, but my voice is from the gods and the gods cannot lie.

Ichtharion:

Is it wise in an age when the gods have lost their power to anger powerful men for the sake of the gods?

Voice-of-the-Gods:

It is wise.

Ichtharion:

We are three men and you are alone with us. Will the gods save you if we want to put you to death and slip away with your body into the jungle?

Voice-of-the-Gods:

If you should do this thing the gods have willed it. If they have not willed it you cannot.

Ichtharion:

We do not wish to do it. Nevertheless you will make this prophecy--you will go before the King and you will say that the gods have spoken and that within three days' time, for the sake of vengeance upon some unknown man who is in this city, they will overthrow all Thek unless every man is departed.

Voice-of-the-Gods:

I will not do it, for the gods cannot lie.

Ichtharion:

Has it not been the custom since unremembered time for a prophet to have two wives?

Voice-of-the-Gods:

Most certainly. It is the law.

   [Ichtharion holds up three fingers.]

What!

Ichtharion:

Three.

Voice-of-the-Gods:

Do not betray me. It was long ago.

Ichtharion:

You will be allowed to serve the gods no more if men know this. The gods will not protect you in this matter for you have offended also against the gods.

Voice-of-the-Gods:

It is worse that the gods should lie. Do not betray me.

Ichtharion:

I go to tell the others what I know.

Voice-of-the-Gods:

I will make the false prophecy.

Ichtharion:

Ah. You have chosen wisely.

Voice-of-the-Gods:

When the gods punish me who make them lie, they will know what punishment to give to you.

Ichtharion:

The gods will not punish us. It is long ago that the gods used to punish men.

Voice-of-the-Gods:

The gods will punish us.

Act II

[Same scene.]

[Same day.]

King Karnos: [pointing off L.]

Look at them now, are they not beautiful? They catch the last rays of the lingering sun. Can you say that the orchids are not beautiful now?

Ichtharion:

Your majesty, we were wrong, they are most beautiful. They tower up from the jungle to take the sun. They are like the diadem of some jubilant king.

King Karnos:

Ah. Now you have come to love the beauty of Thek.

Ichtharion:

Yes, yes, your Majesty, I see it now. I would live in this city always.

King Karnos:

Yes, we will live here always. There is no city lovelier than Thek. Am I not right?

Ludibras:

Your Majesty, no city is like it.

King Karnos:

Ah. I am always right.

Tharmia:

How beautiful is Thek.

Arolind:

Yes, it is like a god.

   [Three notes are stricken on a sonorous gong.]

Whispers: [on]

There has been a prophecy. There has been a prophecy.

King Karnos:

Ah! there has been a prophecy. Bring in the prophet. [Exit attendant.]

   [Enter mournfully with dejected head and walking very slowly Voice-of-the-Gods.]

King Karnos:

You have made a prophecy.

Voice-of-the-Gods:

I have made a prophecy.

King Karnos:

I would hear that prophecy. [A pause.]

Voice-of-the-Gods:

Your Majesty, the gods in three days' time----

King Karnos:

Stop! Is it not usual to begin with certain words? [A pause.]

Voice-of-the-Gods:

It is written and hath been said... that the gods cannot lie.

King Karnos:

That is right.

Voice-of-the-Gods:

That the gods cannot lie.

King Karnos:

Yes. Yes.

Voice-of-the-Gods:

In three days' time the gods will destroy this city for vengeance upon some man, unless all men desert it.

King Karnos:

The gods will destroy Thek!

Voice-of-the-Gods:

Yes.

King Karnos:

When will this happen?

Voice-of-the-Gods:

It must be in three days' time.

King Karnos:

How will it happen?

Voice-of-the-Gods:

Why. It will happen.

King Karnos:

How?

Voice-of-the-Gods:

Why... there will be a sound... as the riving of wood... a sound as of thunder coming up from the ground. A cleft will run like a mouse across the floor. There will be a red light, and then no light at all, and in the darkness Thek shall tumble in.

> [The King sits in deep thought. Exit Prophet slowly; he begins to weep, then casts his cloak over his face. He stretches out his arms to grope his way and is led by the hand. The King sits thinking.]

Tharmia:

Save us, your Majesty.

Arolind:

Save us.

Ichtharion:

We must fly, your Majesty.

Ludibras:

We must escape swiftly.

[The King sits still in silence. He lifts a stick on his right to beat a little silver bell; but puts it down again. At last he lifts it up and strikes the bell. An Attendant enters.]

King Karnos:

Bring back that prophet. [Attendant bows and exits.]

[The King looks thoughtful. The rest have a frightened look. Re-enter Prophet.]

King Karnos:

When the gods prophesy rain in the season of rain, or the death of an old man, we believe them. But when the gods prophesy something incredible and ridiculous, such as happens not nowadays, and hath not been heard of since the fall of Bleth, then our credulity is overtaxed. It is possible that a man should lie; it is not possible that the gods should destroy a city nowadays.

Voice-of-the-Gods:

O King, have mercy.

King Karnos:

What, would you be sent safe away while your King is destroyed by the gods?

Voice-of-the-Gods:

No, no, your Majesty. I would stay in the city, your Majesty. But if the gods do not destroy the city, if the gods have misled me.

King Karnos:

If the gods have misled you they have chosen your doom. Why ask for mercy from me?

Voice-of-the-Gods:

If the gods have misled me, and punish me no further, I ask mercy from you, O King.

King Karnos:

If the gods have misled you, let the gods protect you from my executioner.

1st Sentry: [Laughs aside to 2nd Sentry]

Very witty.

2nd Sentry:

Yes, yes. [Laughs too.]

King Karnos:

If the doom fall not at sunset, why then the executioner----

Voice-of-the-Gods:

Your Majesty!

King Karnos:

No more! No doubt the gods will destroy the whole city at sunset.

   [The sentries titter. The Prophet is led away.]

Ichtharion:

Your Majesty! Is it safe to kill a prophet, even for any guilt? Will not the people----

King Karnos:

Not while he is a prophet; but if he has prophesied falsely his death is due to the gods. The people once even burned a prophet themselves because he had taken three wives.

Ichtharion: [Aside to Ludibras]

It is most unfortunate, but what can we do?

Ludibras: [Aside to Ichtharion]

He will not be killed if he betray us instead.

Ichtharion: [Aside]

Why... that is true.

   [All are whispering.]

King Karnos:

Why do you whisper?

Tharmia:

Your Majesty, we fear that the gods will destroy us all and...

King Karnos:

You do not fear it?

> [Dead silence. A plaintive lament off. Enter the Queen. Her face is pale as paper.]

Queen: [loq.]

O your Majesty. Your Majesty. I have heard the lutanist, I have heard the lutanist.

King Karnos:

She means the lute that is heard by those about to die.

Queen:

I have heard Gog-Owza, the lutanist, playing his lute. And I shall die, O I shall die.

King Karnos:

No. No. No. You have not heard Gog-Owza. Send for her maidens, send for the Queen's maidens.

Queen:

I have heard Gog-Owza playing, and I shall die.

King Karnos:

Hark. Why, I hear it too. That is not Gog-Owza, it is only a man with a lute; I hear it too.

Queen:

O the King hears it too. The King will die. The great King will die. My child will be desolate for the King will die. Mourn, people of the jungle. Mourn, citizens of Thek. And thou, O Barbul-el-Sharnak, O metropolitan city, mourn thou in the midst of the nations, for the great King will die.

King Karnos:

No. No. No. [To oldest present.] Listen you. Do you not hear it?

The Oldest:

Yes, your Majesty.

King Karnos:

You see it is a real lute. That is no spirit playing.

Queen:

O but he is old; in a few days he will die; it is Gog-Owza, and the King will die.

King Karnos:

No, no, it is only a man. Look out of the window there. [To any Young Man.]

The Young Man:

It is dark, your Majesty, and I cannot see.

Queen:

It is the spirit Gog-Owza.

The Young Man:

I can hear the music clearly.

King Karnos:

He is young.

Queen:

The young are always in danger; they go about among swords. He will die too and the great King and I. In a few days we will be buried.

King Karnos:

Let us all listen; we cannot all die in a few days' time.

Tharmia:

I hear it clearly.

Queen:

Women are blossoms in the hand of Death. They are often close to Death. She will die too.

All:

I hear it. I hear it. And I. And I. And I. It is only a man with a lute.

Queen: [pacified]

I should like to see him, then I should know for certain.

   [She looks out of the casement.]

No, it is too dark.

King Karnos:

We will call the man if you wish it.

Queen:

Yes, I shall be easy then, and then I shall sleep.

   [King instructs Attendants to enquire without. Queen at window still.]

King Karnos:

It is some man down by the river playing his lute. I am told that sometimes a man will play all night.

Tharmia: [Aside]

That's their amusement here.

Arolind: [Aside]

Well, really, its almost all the music we get.

Tharmia: [Aside]

It really is.

Arolind: [Aside]

O how I cry for the golden Hall of Song in Barbul-el-Sharnak. I think it would almost hold the city of Thek.

   [Re-enter Attendant]

Attendant:

It is only a common lute, your Majesty. All hear it except one man.
King Karnos:

All except one, did you say? Ah, thank you.

   [To Queen at window.]

It is only a common lute.

Queen:

One man did not hear it. Who was he? Where is he? Why didn't he?

Attendant:

He was riding back again to Barbul-el-Sharnak. He was just starting. He said he did not hear it.

Queen:

Oh, send for him here.

Attendant:

He is gone, your Majesty.

Queen:

Overtake him quick. Overtake him.

　　[Exit Attendant.]

Tharmia: [Aside to Arolind]

I wish that I were going back to Barbul-el-Sharnak.

Arolind:

O to be again at the centre of the world!

Tharmia:

Were we not talking of the golden hall?

Arolind:

Ah, yes. How lovely it was! How beautiful it was when the King was there and strange musicians came from the heathen lands with huge plumes in their hair, and played on instruments that we did not know.

Tharmia:

The Queen was better then. The music eased her.

Arolind:

This lute player is making her quite mad.

Tharmia:

Well. Well. No wonder. He has a mournful sound. Listen!

Arolind:

Do not let us listen. It makes me feel cold.
Tharmia:

He cannot play like Nagra or dear Trehannion. It is because we have heard Trehannion that we do not like to listen.

Arolind:

I do not like to listen because I feel cold.

Tharmia:

We feel cold because the Queen has opened the casement.

King Karnos: [To Attendant]

Find the man that is playing the lute and give him this and let him cease to play upon his lute.

　[Exit Attendant]

Ichtharion:

Hark! He is playing still.

King Karnos:

Yes, we all hear him; it is only a man.

　[To another or same Attendant]

Let him stop playing.

Attendant:

Yes, your Majesty. [Exit]

　[Enter an Attendant with another]

Attendant:

This is the man that does not hear the lute.

King Karnos:

Ah. You are deaf, then, are you not?

Man:

No, your Majesty.

King Karnos:

You hear me clearly?

Man:

Yes, your Majesty.

King Karnos:

Listen! ...Now you hear the lute?

Man:

No, your Majesty.
King Karnos:

Who sent you to Barbul-el-Sharnak?

Man:

The captain of the camel-guard sent me, your Majesty.

King Karnos:

Then go and never return. You are deaf and also a fool. [To himself] The Queen will not sleep. [To Another] Bring music, bring music quickly. [Muttering] The Queen will not sleep.

[The man bows low and departs. He says farewell to a sentry. The Queen leans from the casement muttering. Music heard off.]

Queen:

Ah, that is earthly music, but of that other tune I have a fear.

King Karnos:

We have all heard it. Comfort yourself. Calm yourself.

Queen:

One man does not hear it.

King Karnos:

But he has gone away. We all hear it now.

Queen:

I wish that I could see him.

King Karnos:

A man is a small thing and the night very large and full of wonders. You may well not see him.

Queen:

I should like to see him. Why cannot I see him?

King Karnos:

I have sent the camel-guard to search for him and to stop him playing his lute.

   [To Ichtharion]

Do not let the Queen know about this prophecy. She would think... I do not know what she would think.

Ichtharion:

No, your Majesty.

King Karnos:

The Queen has a very special fear of the gods.

Ichtharion:

Yes, your Majesty.

Queen:

You speak of me?

King Karnos:

O no. We speak of the gods.

   [The earthly music ceases.]

Queen:

O do not speak of the gods. The gods are very terrible; all the dooms that shall ever be come forth from the gods. In misty windings of the wandering hills they forge the future even as on an anvil. The future frightens me.

King Karnos:

Call the Queen's maidens. Send quickly for her maidens. Do not let the future frighten you.

Queen:

Men laugh at the gods; they often laugh at the gods. I am more sure that the gods laugh too. It is dreadful to think of the laughter of the gods. O the lute! the lute! How clearly I hear the lute. But you all hear it? Do you not? You swear that you all hear it?

King Karnos:

Yes, yes. We all hear the lute. It is only a man playing.

Queen:

I wish I could see him. Then I should know that he was only a man and not Gog-Owza, most terrible of the gods. I should be able to sleep then.

King Karnos: [Soothingly]

Yes, yes.

[Enter Attendant]

Here comes the man that I have sent to find him. You have found the lute player. Tell the queen that you have found the lute player.

Attendant:

The camel-guard have searched, your Majesty, and cannot find any man that is playing a lute.

[Curtain]

Act III

[Three days elapse.]

Tharmia:

We have done too much. We have done too much. Our husbands will be put to death. The prophet will betray them and they will be put to death.

Arolind:

O what shall we do?

Tharmia:

It would have been better for us to have been clothed with rags than to bring our husbands to death by what we have done.

Arolind:

We have done much and we have angered a king, and (who knows!) we may have angered even the gods.

Tharmia:

Even the gods! We are become like Helen. When my mother was a child she saw her once. She says she was the quietest and gentlest of creatures and wished only to be loved, and yet because of her there was a war for four or five years at Troy, and the city was burned which had remarkable towers; and some of the gods of the Greeks took her side, my mother says, and some she says were against her, and they quarrelled upon Olympus where they live, and all because of Helen.

Arolind:

O don't, don't. It frightens me. I only want to be prettily dressed and see my husband happy.

Tharmia:

Have you seen the prophet?

Arolind:

Oh yes, I have seen him. He walks about the palace. He is free but cannot escape.

Tharmia:

What does he look like? Has he a frightened look?

Arolind:

He mutters as he walks. Sometimes he weeps; and then he puts his cloak over his face.

Tharmia:

I fear that he will betray them.

Arolind:

I do not trust a prophet. He is the go-between of gods and men. They are so far apart. How can he be true to both?

Tharmia:

This prophet is false to the gods. It is a hateful thing for a prophet to prophesy falsely.

   [Prophet walks across hanging his head and muttering.]
Prophet:

The gods have spoken a lie. The gods have spoken a lie. Can all their vengeance ever atone for this?

Tharmia:

He spoke of vengeance.

Arolind:

O he will betray them.

   [They weep. Enter the Queen.]

Queen:

Why do you weep? Ah, you are going to die. You heard the death-lute. You do well to weep.

Tharmia:

No, your Majesty. It is the man that has played for the last three days. We all heard him.

Queen:

Three days. Yes, it is three days. Gog-Owza plays no longer than three days. Gog-Owza grows weary then. He has given his message and he will go away.

Tharmia:

We have all heard him, your Majesty, except the deaf young man that went back to Barbul-el-Sharnak. We hear him now.

Queen: Yes! But nobody has seen him yet. My maidens have searched for him but they have not found him.

Tharmia:

Your Majesty, my husband heard him, and Ludibras, and while they live we know there is nothing to fear. If the King grew angry with them--because of any idle story that some jealous man might tell--some criminal wishing to postpone his punishment--if the King were to grow angry with them they would open their veins; they would never survive his anger. Then we should all of us say, "Perhaps it was Gog-Owza that Ichtharion or Ludibras heard."

Queen:

The King will never grow angry with Ichtharion or Ludibras.

Tharmia:

Your Majesty would not sleep if the King grew angry with them.

Queen:

Oh, no. I should not sleep; it would be terrible.

Tharmia:

Your Majesty would be wakeful all night long and cry.
Queen:

Oh, yes. I should not sleep; I should cry all night. [Exit]

Arolind:

She has no influence with the King.

Tharmia:

No. But he hates to hear her cry all night.

　[Enter Ichtharion]

I am sure that the prophet will betray you. But we have spoken to the Queen. We have told her it would be dreadful if the King were to grow angry with you, and she things she will cry all night if he is angry.

Ichtharion:

Poor frightened brain! How strong are little fancies! She should be a beautiful Queen. But she goes about white and crying, in fear of the gods. The gods, that are no more than shadows in the moonlight. Man's fear rises weird and large in all this mystery and makes a shadow of himself upon the ground and Man jumps and says "the gods." Why they are less than shadows; we have seen shadows, we have not seen the gods.

Tharmia:

O do not speak like that. There used to be gods. They overthrew Bleth dreadfully. And if they still live on in the dark of the hills, why, they might hear your words.

Ichtharion:

Why! you grow frightened, too. Do not be frightened. We will go and speak with the prophet, while you follow the Queen; be much with her, and do not let her forget that she will cry if the King should be angry with us.

Arolind:

I am almost afraid when I am with the Queen; I do not like to be with her.

Tharmia:

She could not hurt us; she is afraid of all things.

Arolind:

She makes me have huge fears of prodigious things.

   [Exeunt Tharmia and Arolind.]

[Enter Ludibras.]

Ludibras:

The prophet is coming this way.

Ichtharion:

Sit down. We must speak with him. He will betray us.

Ludibras:

Why should the prophet betray us?

Ichtharion:

Because the guilt of the false prophecy is not his guilt; it is ours; and the King may spare him if he tells him that. Again, he mutters of vengeance as he walks; many have told me.

Ludibras:

The King will not spare him even if he betrays us. It was he that spoke the false prophecy to the King.

Ichtharion:

The King does not in his heart believe in the gods. It is for cheating him that the prophet is to die. But if he knows we had planned it----

Ludibras:

What can we say to the prophet?

Ichtharion:

Why, we can say nothing. But we can learn what he will do from what he says to us.

Ludibras:

Here he is. We must remember everything that he says.

Ichtharion:

Watch his eyes.

   [Enter the Prophet, his eyes concealed by his cloak.]

Ichtharion and Ludibras:

The gods are good.

Voice-of-the-Gods:

They are benignant.

Ichtharion:

I am much to blame. I am very much to blame.

Ludibras:

We trust that the King will relent.

Ichtharion:

He often relents at sunset; he looks out over the orchids in the evening. They are very beautiful then, and if he is angry his anger passes away just when the cool breeze comes at the set of sun.

Ludibras:

He is sure to relent at sunset.

Ichtharion:

Do not be angry. I am indeed to blame. Do not be angry.

Voice-of-the-Gods:

I do not wish the King to relent at sunset.

Ichtharion:

Do not be unhappy.

Voice-of-the-Gods:

I say to you that I have betrayed the gods.

Ichtharion:

Listen to me. Do not be so unhappy. There are no gods. Everybody knows that there are no gods. The King knows it.

Voice-of-the-Gods:

You have heard their prophet lie and believe that the gods are dead?

Ludibras:

There are indeed no gods. It is well known.

Voice-of-the-Gods:

There are gods, and they have a vengeance even for you. Listen and I will tell you what it shall be. Aye and for you also... Listen!... No, no, they are silent in the gloom of the hills. They have not spoken to me since I lied.

Ichtharion:

You are right; the gods will punish us. It is natural that they should not speak just now; but they will certainly punish us. It is not therefore necessary for any man to avenge himself upon us, even though there were any cause.

Voice-of-the-Gods:

It is not necessary.

Ichtharion:

Indeed, it might even further anger the gods if a man should be before them to punish us.

Voice-of-the-Gods:

The gods are very swift; no man outruns them.

Ludibras:

A man would be rash to attempt to.

Voice-of-the-Gods:

The sun is falling low. I will leave you now, for I have ever loved the sun at evening. I go to watch it drop through the gilded clouds, and make a wonder of familiar things. After the sunset, night, and after an evil deed, the vengeance of the gods. [Exit R.]

Ludibras: [with contemptuous wonder]

He really believes in the gods.

Ichtharion:

He is as mad as the Queen; we must humour his madness if we ever see him more. I think that all will be well.

    [An executioner steals after the Prophet; he is dressed in crimson satin to the knees; he wears a leather belt and carries the axe of his trade.]

Ludibras:

His voice was angry as he went away. I fear he may yet betray us.

Ichtharion:

It is not likely. He thinks that the gods will punish us.

Ludibras:

How long will he think so? The Queen's fancies change thrice an hour.

Ichtharion:

The executioner keeps very close to him now. He comes closer every hour. There is not much time for him to change his fancies.

Ludibras:

He has the will to betray us if that fancy leaves him.
Ichtharion:

The executioner is very eager for him. He invented a new stroke lately, but he has not had a man since we came to Thek.

Ludibras:

I do not like an eager executioner--the King sees him and it makes him think...

Ichtharion:

Look how low the sun is; he has no time to betray us. The King is not yet here.

Ludibras:

He is coming.

Ichtharion:

But the prophet is not here.

Ludibras:

No, he is not yet come.

   [Enter the King.]

King Karnos:

The Queen's maidens have persuaded her that there is nothing to fear. They are quite excellent; they shall dance before me. The Queen will sleep; they are quite excellent. Ah, Ichtharion. Come to me, Ichtharion.

Ludibras:

Why does the King send for you?

King Karnos:

You were wrong, Ichtharion.

Ichtharion:

Your Majesty!

[Ludibras watches.]

King Karnos:

You were wrong to think that Thek is not very lovely.

Ichtharion:

Yes, I was wrong and I am much to blame.

King Karnos:

Yes, it is very beautiful at evening. I will watch them go down over the orchids. I will never see Barbul-el-Sharnak any more. I will sit and watch the sun go down on the orchids till it is gone and all their colours fade.

Ichtharion:

It is very beautiful now. How still it is! I have never seen so still a sunset before.

King Karnos:

It is like a picture done by a dying painter, full of a beautiful colour. Even if all these orchids died to-night yet their beauty is an indestructible memory.

Ludibras: [Aside to Ichtharion]

The prophet is coming this way.

Ichtharion:

Your Majesty, the prophet walks about in the palace, and the executioner is close behind him. If the Queen saw him and the executioner would it not trouble her? Were it not better that he should be killed at once? Shall I whistle for the executioner?

King Karnos:

Not now. I said at sunset.

Ichtharion:

Your Majesty, it is merciful to kill a man before the set of the sun. For it is natural in a man to love the sun. But to see it set and to know that it will not come again is even a second death. It would be merciful to kill him now.

King Karnos:

I have said--at sunset. It were unjust to kill him before his prophecy is proven false.

Ichtharion:

But, your Majesty, we know that it is false. He also knows it.

King Karnos:

He shall die at sunset.

Ludibras:

Your Majesty, the prophet will pray for life if he is not killed now.
It would be pity to grant it.

King Karnos:

Is not a King's word death? I have said he shall die at sunset.

  [Enter Prophet. The Executioner creeps along close behind him.]

Voice-of-the-Gods:

O the gods are about to have lied. The gods will have lied. I have prophesied falsely and the gods will have lied. My death cannot atone for it nor the punishment of others.

  [Ichtharion and Ludibras start.]

Ichtharion:

He will betray us yet.

Voice-of-the-Gods:

O why did you let your voice come through my lips? O why did you allow your voice to lie? For centuries it has been said from city to city, "The gods cannot lie." The nomads have known it out upon the plains. The mountaineers have known it near the dawn. That is all over now. O King, let me die at once. For I have prophesied falsely and at sunset the gods will lie.

King Karnos:

It is not sunset yet. No doubt you have spoken truly.

[Enter Queen.]

How well the Queen looks. Her maidens are quite excellent.

Ludibras: [To Ichtharion]

There is something a little dreadful in seeing the Queen so calm. She is like a windless sunset in the Winter before a hurricane comes and the snow swirls up before it over the world.

Ichtharion:

I do not like calm sunsets; they make me think that something is going to happen. Yes, the Queen is very quiet; she will sleep to-night.

Queen:

I am not frightened any longer. All the wild fancies of my brain have left it. I have often troubled you with little fears. Now they are all at rest and I am afraid no longer.

King Karnos:

That is good; I am very glad. You will sleep tonight.

Queen:

Sleep. Why--yes, I shall sleep. O yes, we shall all sleep.

King Karnos:

Your maidens have told you that there is nothing to fear.

Queen:

Nothing to fear? No, no more little fears to trouble me.

King Karnos:

They have told you there is nothing at all to fear. Indeed there is nothing.

Queen:

No more little fears. There is one great fear.

King Karnos:

A great fear! Why, what is it?

Queen:

I must not say. For you have often soothed me when I was frightened, and it were not well for me to trouble you at the last.

King Karnos:

What is your fear? Shall I send again for your maidens?

Queen:

No, it is not my fear. It is all men's fear if they knew.

King Karnos: [glancing round]

Ah, you have seen my man in red. I will send him away. I will----

Queen:

No, no. My fear is not earthly. I am not afraid of little things any more.

King Karnos:

Why, what is it then?

Queen:

I do not quite know. But you know how I have ever feared the gods. The gods are going to do some dreadful thing.

King Karnos:

Believe me; the gods do nothing nowadays.

Queen:

You have indeed been very good to me. It seems a little while since the camels came to Argun-Zeerith by the iris marshes, the camels with the gold-hung palanquin, and the bells above their heads, high up in the air, the silver bridal bells. It seems a very little while ago. I did not know how swift the end would come.

King Karnos:

What end? To whom is the end coming?

Queen:

Do not be troubled. We should not let Fate trouble us. The World and its daily cares, ah, they are frightful: but Fate--I smile at Fate. Fate cannot hurt us if we smile at it.

King Karnos:

What end do you say is coming?

Queen:

I do not know. Something that has been shall soon be no more.

King Karnos:

No, no. Look upon Thek. It is built of rock and our palace is all of marble. Time has not scratched it with six centuries. Six tearing centuries with all their claws. We are throned on gold and founded upon marble. Death will some day find me, indeed, but I am young. Sire after sire of mine has died in Barbul-el-Sharnak or in Thek, but has left our dynasty laughing sheer in the face of Time from over these age-old walls.

Queen:

Say farewell to me now, lest something happen.

King Karnos:

No, no, we will not say unhappy things.

Executioner:

The sun has set.

King Karnos:

Not yet. The jungle hides it. It is not yet set. Look at the beautiful light upon the orchids. For how long they have flashed their purple on the gleaming walls of Thek. For how long they will flash there on our immortal palace, immortal in marble and immortal in song. Ah, how the colour changes.

   [To the Executioner]

The sun is set. Take him away.
   [To the Queen]

It is he whose end you foresaw.

   [The Executioner grips the Prophet by the arm.]

Voice-of-the-Gods:

The gods have lied!

King Karnos:

The jungle is sinking! It has fallen into the earth!

   [The Queen smiles a little, holding his hand.]

The city is falling in! The houses are rolling towards us!

   [Thunder off.]

Ichtharion:

They are coming up like a wave and darkness is coming with them.

>[Loud and prolonged thunder. Flashes of red light and then total darkness. A little light comes back, showing recumbent figures, shattered pillars and rocks of white marble.]

>[The Prophet's back is broken, but he raises the fore-part of his body for a moment.]

Voice-of-the-Gods: [triumphantly]

They have not lied!

Ichtharion:

O, I am killed.

>[Laughter heard off.]

Someone is laughing. Laughing even in Thek! Why, the whole city is shattered.

>[The laughter grows demoniac.]

What is that dreadful sound?

Voice-of-the-Gods:

It is the laughter of the gods that cannot lie, going back to their hills.

[He dies.]

[Curtain]

The Queen's Enemies

Dramatis Personae

The Queen
Ackazarpses (her handmaid)
Prince Rhadamandaspes
Prince Zophernes
The Priest of Horus
The King of the Four Countries
The Twin Dukes of Ethiopia
Tharni, Tharrabas, Harlee (Slaves)
Slaves.

Scene: An underground temple in Egypt.

Time: The Sixth Dynasty.

> [The Curtain rises on darkness in both parts of the stage. Two Slaves appear with tapers on the steps. As they go down the steps, they light the torches that are clamped against the wall, with their tapers. Afterwards when they come to the temple they light the torches there till they are all lit. The two Slaves are Tharni and Tharrabas.]

Tharrabas:

Is it much further, Tharni?

Tharni:

I think not, Tharrabas.

Tharrabas:

A dank and terrible place.

Tharni:

It is not much further.

Tharrabas:

Why does the Queen banquet in so fearful a place?

Tharni:

I know not. She banquets with her enemies.

Tharrabas:

In the land from which I was taken we do not banquet with our enemies.

Tharni:

No? The Queen will banquet with her enemies.

Tharrabas:

Why? Know you why?

Tharni:

It is the way of the Queen.

   [Silence.]

Tharrabas:

The door, Tharni, we have come to the door!

Tharni:

Yes, that's the Temple.
Tharrabas:

Surely a grim place.

Tharni:

The banquet is prepared. We light these torches, that is all.

Tharrabas:

Unto whom is it holy?

Tharni:

They say to the Nile once. I know not to whom it is holy now.

Tharrabas:

So Nile has left it?

Tharni:

They say they worship him in this place no longer.

Tharrabas:

And if I were holy Nile I also would stay up there [pointing] in the sunlight.

 [He suddenly sees the huge misshapen bulk of Harlee.]

Oh-h-h!

Harlee:

Urh

Tharni:

Why, it's Harlee.

Tharrabas:

I thought you were some fearful, evil god.

 [Harlee laughs. He remains leaning on his great iron bar.]

Tharni:

He waits here for the Queen.

Tharrabas:

What sinister need could she have of Harlee?

Tharni:

I know not. You wait for the Queen, Harlee?

   [Harlee nods.]

Tharrabas:

I would not banquet here. Not with a Queen.

   [Harlee laughs long.]
Tharrabas:

Our work is done. Come. Let us leave this place.

   [Exeunt Tharrabas and Tharni up the steps.]

   [The Queen appears with her handmaid, Ackazarpses, coming down the steps. Her handmaid holds her train. They enter the temple.]

Queen:

Ah. All is ready.

Ackazarpses:

No, no, Illustrious Lady. Nothing is ready. Your raiment--we must fasten it here [shoulder], and then the bow in your hair.

   [She begins to titivate the Queen.]

Queen:

Ackazarpses, Ackazarpses, I cannot bear to have enemies.

Ackazarpses:

Indeed, Illustrious Lady, it is wrong that you should have enemies. One so delicate, so slender and withal so beautiful should never have a foe.

Queen:

If the gods could understand they would never permit it.

Ackazarpses:

I have poured out dark wine to them, I have offered them fat, indeed, I have often offered them savoury things. I have said: The Queen should not have enemies; she is too delicate, too fair. But they will not understand.

Queen:

If they could see my tears they would never permit such woes to be borne by one small woman. But they only look at men and their horrible wars. Why must men slay one another and make horrible war?

Ackazarpses:

I blame your enemies, Illustrious Lady, more than the gods. Why should they trouble you who are so fair and so easily hurt by their anger? It was but a little territory you took from them. How much better to lose a little territory than to be unmannerly and unkind.

Queen:

O speak not of the territory. I know naught of these things. They say my Captains took it. How should I know? O why will they be my enemies?

Ackazarpses:

You are most fair to-night, Illustrious Lady.

Queen:

I must needs be fair to-night.

Ackazarpses:

Indeed you are most fair.

Queen:

A little more perfume, Ackazarpses.

Ackazarpses:

I will tie the coloured bow more evenly.

Queen:

O they will never look at it. They will not know if it is orange or blue. I shall weep if they do not look at it. It is a pretty bow.

Ackazarpses:

Calm yourself, lady! They will be here soon.

Queen:

Indeed I think they are very close to me now, for I feel myself trembling.

Ackazarpses:

You must not tremble, Illustrious Lady; you must not tremble.

Queen:

They are such terrible men, Ackazarpses.

Ackazarpses:

But you must not tremble, for your raiment is now perfect; yet if you tremble, alas! who may say how it will hang?

Queen:

They are such huge, terrible men.

Ackazarpses:

O the raiment, the raiment; you must not, you must not!

Queen:

O I cannot bear it. I cannot bear it. There is Rhadamandaspes, that huge, fierce soldier, and the terrible Priest of Horus, and... and... O I cannot see them, I cannot see them.

Ackazarpses:

Lady, you have invited them.

Queen:

O say I am ill, say I am sick of a fever.

Quick, quick, say I have some swift fever and cannot see them.

Ackazarpses:

Illustrious Lady----

Queen:

Quick, for I cannot bear it.

   [Exit Ackazarpses.]

Queen:

O, I cannot bear to have enemies.

Ackazarpses:

Lady, they are here.

Queen:

O what shall we do?... Set this bow higher upon my head so that it must be seen. [Ackazarpses does so.] The pretty bow.

> [She continues to look in a hand mirror. A Slave descends the stairs. Then Rhadamandaspes and Zophernes. Rhadamandaspes and Zophernes stop; the Slave stops lower down.]

Zophernes:

For the last time, Rhadamandaspes, consider. Even yet we may turn back.

Rhadamandaspes:

She had no guards outside nor was there any hiding place for them. There was the empty plain and the Nile only.

Zophernes:

Who knows what she may have in this dark temple?

Rhadamandaspes:

It is small and the stairway narrow; our friends are close behind us. We could hold these steps with our swords against all her men.

Zophernes:

True. They are narrow steps. Yet... Rhadamandaspes, I do not fear man or god or even woman, yet when I saw the letter this woman sent bidding us banquet with her I felt that it was not well that we should come.

Rhadamandaspes:

She said that she would love us though we were her enemies.

Zophernes:

It is not natural to love one's enemies.

Rhadamandaspes:

She is much swayed by whims. They sway her as the winds in spring sway flowers--this way and that. This is one of her whims.
Zophernes:

I do not trust her whims.

Rhadamandaspes:

They name you Zophernes, giver of good counsel, therefore I will turn back because you counsel it, though I would fain go down and banquet with this little playful lady.

[They turn and mount.]

Zophernes:

Believe me, Rhadamandaspes, it is better. I think that if you had gone down these steps we scarcely should have seen the sky again.

Rhadamandaspes:

Well, well, we turn back, though I would fain have humoured the Queen's whim. But look. The others come. We cannot turn back. There comes the Priest of Horus; we must go to the banquet now.

Zophernes:

So be it.

   [They descend.]

Rhadamandaspes:

We will be circumspect. If she has men in there we return at once.

Zophernes:

So be it.

   [The Slave opens the door.]

Slave:

The Princes Rhadamandaspes and Zophernes.

Queen:

Welcome, Illustrious Princes.

Rhadamandaspes:

Greeting.

Queen:

O you have brought your sword!

Rhadamandaspes:

I have brought my sword.

Queen:

O but it is so terrible, your great sword.

Zophernes:

We always carry our swords.
Queen:

O but you do not need them. If you have come to kill me your great hands are enough. But why do you bring your swords?

Rhadamandaspes:

Illustrious Lady, we do not come to kill you.

Queen:

To your post, Harlee.

Zophernes:

What are this Harlee and his post?

Ackazarpses:

Do not tremble, Illustrious Lady, indeed you must not tremble.

Queen:

He is but a fisherman; he lives upon the Nile. He nets fish; indeed he is nothing.

Zophernes:

For what is your great bar of iron, Slave?

   [Harlee opens his mouth showing that he is tongueless. Exit.]

Rhadamandaspes:

Ugh! They have burned out his tongue.

Zophernes:

He goes on secret errands.

   [Enter Second Slave.]

Second Slave:

The Priest of Horus.

Queen:

Welcome, holy companion of the gods.

Priest of Horus:

Greeting.

Third Slave:

The King of the Four Countries.

    [She and he make obeisance.]

Fourth Slave:

The Twin Dukes of Ethiopia.

King of the Four Countries:

We are all met.

Priest of Horus:

All that have warred against her Captains.

Queen:

O speak not of my Captains. It troubles me to hear of violent men. But you have been my enemies, and I cannot bear to have enemies. Therefore I have asked you to banquet with me.

Priest of Horus:

And we have come.

Queen:

O look not so sternly at me. I cannot bear to have enemies. When I have enemies I do not sleep. Is it not so, Ackazarpses?

Ackazarpses:

Indeed, the Illustrious Lady has suffered much.

Queen:

O Ackazarpses, why should I have enemies?

Ackazarpses:

After to-night you will sleep, Illustrious Lady.

Queen:

Why, yes, for we shall all be friends; shall we not, princes? Let us be seated.

Rhadamandaspes:

[To Zophernes.] There is no other doorway. That is well.

Zophernes:

Why, no, there is not. Yet what is that great hole that is full of darkness?

Rhadamandaspes:

Only one man at a time could come that way. We are safe from man or beast. Nothing could enter that way for our swords.

Queen:

I pray you be seated.

   [They seat themselves cautiously, she standing watching them.]

Zophernes:

There are no servitors.

Queen:

Are there not viands before you, Prince Zophernes, or are there too few fruits that you should blame me?

Zophernes:

I do not blame you.

Queen:

I fear you blame me with your fierce eyes.

Zophernes:

I do not blame you.

Queen:

O my enemies, I would have you kind to me. And indeed there are no servitors, for I know what evil things you think of me----

A Duke of Ethiopia:

No, Queen, indeed we think no evil of you.

Queen:

Ah, but you think terrible things.

Priest of Horus:

We think no evil of you, Illustrious Lady.
Queen:

I feared that if I had servitors you would think... you would say, "This wicked Queen, our enemy, will bid them attack us while we feast."

   [First Duke of Ethiopia furtively hands food to his Slave standing behind him, who tastes it.]

Though you do not know how I dread the sight of blood, and indeed I would never bid them do such a thing. The sight of blood is shocking.

Priest of Horus:

We trust you, Illustrious Lady.

   [He does the same with his Slave.]

Queen:

And for miles around this temple and all along this river I have said, "Let there be no man." I have commanded and there are not. Will you not trust me now?

[Zophernes does the same and all the guests, one by one.]

Priest of Horus:

Indeed, we trust you.

Queen:

And you, Prince Zophernes, with your fierce eyes that so frighten me, will you not trust me?

Zophernes:

O Queen, it is part of the art of war to be well prepared when in an enemy's country, and we have been so long at war with your Captains that we perforce remember some of the art. It is not that we do not trust you.

Queen:

I am all alone with my handmaid and none will trust me! O Ackazarpses, I am frightened: what if my enemies should slay me and carry me up, and cast my body into the lonely Nile.

Ackazarpses:

No, no, Illustrious Lady. They will not harm you. They do not know how their fierce looks distress you. They do not know how delicate you are.

Priest of Horus: [to Ackazarpses]

Indeed we trust the Queen and none would harm her.

   [Ackazarpses soothes the Queen.]

Rhadamandaspes: [to Zophernes]

I think we do wrong to doubt her, seeing she is alone.

Zophernes: [to Rhadamandaspes]

Yet I would that the banquet were over.

Queen: [to Ackazarpses and the Priest of Horus, but audible to all]

Yet they do not eat the food that I set before them.

Duke of Ethiopia:

In Ethiopia when we feast with queens it is our custom not to eat at once but to await the Queen till she has eaten.

Queen: [Eats.]

Behold then, I have eaten.

   [She looks at the Priest of Horus.]

Priest of Horus:

It has been the custom of all that held my office, from the time when there went on earth the children of the Moon, never to eat till the food is dedicate, by our sacred signs, to the gods. [He begins to wave his hands over the food.]

Queen:

The King of the Four Countries does not eat. And you, Prince Rhadamandaspes, you have given royal wine unto your slave.

Rhadamandaspes:

O Queen, it is the custom of our dynasty... and has indeed long been so,... as many say,... that the noble should not feast till the base have feasted, reminding us that our bodies even as the humble bodies of the base----

Queen:

Why do you thus watch your slave, Prince Rhadamandaspes?

Rhadamandaspes:

Even to remind myself that I have done as our dynasty doth.

Queen:

Alas for me, Ackazarpses, they will not feast with me, but mock me because I am little and alone. O I shall not sleep to-night, I shall not sleep. [She weeps.]

Ackazarpses:

Yes, yes, Illustrious Lady, you shall sleep. Be patient and all shall be well and you will sleep.

Rhadamandaspes:

But Queen, Queen, we are about to eat.

Duke of Ethiopia:

Yes, yes, indeed we do not mock you.
King of Four Countries:

We do not mock you, Queen.

Priest of Horus:

They do not mean to mock you.

Queen:

They... give my food to slaves.

Priest of Horus:

That was a mistake.

Queen:

It was... no mistake.

Priest of Horus:

The slaves were hungry.

Queen: [still weeping]

They believe I would poison them.

Priest of Horus:

No, no, Illustrious Lady, they do not believe that.

Queen:

They believe I would poison them.

Ackazarpses: [comforting her]

O hush, hush. They do not mean to be so cruel.

Priest of Horus:

They do not believe you would poison them. But they do not know if the meat was killed with a poisonous arrow or if an asp may have inadvertently bitten the fruit. These things may happen, but they do not believe you would poison them.

Queen:

They believe I would poison them.

Rhadamandaspes:

No; Queen, see, we eat.

   [They hastily whisper to slaves.]

1st Duke of Ethiopia:

We eat your viands, Queen.

2nd Duke of Ethiopia:

We drink your wine.

King of Four Countries:

We eat your good pomegranates and Egyptian grapes.

Zophernes:

We eat.

   [They all eat.]

Priest of Horus: [smiling affably]

I too eat of your excellent banquet, O Queen.

   [He peels a fruit slowly, glancing constantly at the others. Meanwhile the catches in the Queen's breath grow fewer, she begins to dry her eyes.]

Ackazarpses: [in her ear]

They eat.

   [Ackazarpses lifts her head and watches them.]

Queen:

Perhaps the wine is poisoned.

Priest of Horus:

No, no, Illustrious Lady.

Queen:

Perhaps the grape was cut by a poisoned arrow.

Priest of Horus:

But indeed... indeed...

   [Queen drinks from his cup.]

Queen:

Will you not drink my wine?

Priest of Horus:

I drink to our continued friendship.

[He drinks.]

A Duke of Ethiopia:

Our continued friendship!

Priest of Horus:

There has been no true enmity. We misunderstood the Queen's armies.

Rhadamandaspes: [to Zophernes]

We have wronged the Queen. The wine's not poisoned. Let us drink to her.

Zophernes:

So be it.

Rhadamandaspes:

We drink to you, Queen.

Zophernes:

We drink.

Queen:

The flagon, Ackazarpses.

[Ackazarpses brings it. The Queen pours it into her cup.]

Fill up your goblets from the flagon, princes. [She drinks.]

Rhadamandaspes:

We wronged you, Queen. It is a blessed wine.

Queen:

It is an ancient wine and grew in Lesbos, looking from Mytelene to the South. Ships brought it overseas and up this river to gladden the hearts of man in holy Egypt. But to me it brings no joy.

Duke of Ethiopia:

It is a happy wine, Queen.
Queen:

I have been thought a poisoner.

Priest of Horus:

Indeed, none has thought that, Illustrious Lady.

Queen:

You have all thought it.

Rhadamandaspes:

We ask your pardon, Queen.

King of Four Countries:

We ask your pardon.

Duke of Ethiopia:

Indeed we erred.

Zophernes: [rising]

We have eaten your fruits and drunk your wine; and we have asked your pardon. Let us now depart in amity.

Queen:

No, no! No, no! You must not go! I shall say... "They are my enemies still," and I shall not sleep. I that cannot bear to have enemies.
Zophernes:

Let us depart in all amity.

Queen:

O will you not feast with me?

Zophernes:

We have feasted.

Rhadamandaspes:

No, no, Zophernes. Do you not see? The Queen takes it to heart.

   [Zophernes sits down.]

Queen:

O feast with me a little longer and make merry, and be my enemies no more. Rhadamandaspes, there is some country eastwards towards Assyria, is there not? I do not know its name--a country which your dynasty claims of me...

Zophernes:

Ha!

Rhadamandaspes: [resignedly]

We have lost it.

Queen:

...and for whose sake you are my enemy and your fierce uncle, Prince Zophernes.

Rhadamandaspes:

We fought somewhat with your armies, Queen. But indeed it was but to practise the military art.

Queen:

I will call my Captains to me. I will call them down from their high places and reprove them and bid them give the country back to you that lies eastwards towards Assyria. Only you shall tarry here at the feast and forget you ever were my enemies... forget...

Rhadamandaspes:

Queen...! Queen...! It was my mother's country as a child.

Queen:

You will not leave me alone then here to-night.

Rhadamandaspes:

No, most royal lady.

Queen: [to King of Four Countries who appears about to depart]

And in the matter of the merchant men that trade amongst the isles, they shall offer spices at your feet, not at mine, and the men of the isles shall offer goats to your gods.

King of Four Countries:

Most generous Queen... indeed...

Queen:

But you will not leave my banquet and go unfriendly away.

King of Four Countries:

No, Queen... [He drinks.]

Queen: [she looks at the Twin Dukes amiably]

All Ethiopia shall be yours, down to the unknown kingdoms of the beasts.

1st Duke of Ethiopia:

Queen.

2nd Duke of Ethiopia:

Queen. We drink to the glory of your throne.

Queen:

Stay then and feast with me. For not to have enemies is the beggar's joy; and I have looked from windows long and long, envying those that go their way in rags. Stay with me, dukes and princes.

Priest of Horus:

Illustrious Lady, the generosity of your royal heart has given the gods much joy.

Queen: [smiles at him.]

Thank you.

Priest of Horus:

Er... in the matter of the tribute due to Horus from all the people of Egypt...

Queen:

It is yours.

Priest of Horus:

Illustrious Lady.

Queen:

I will take none of it. Use it how you will.

Priest of Horus:

The gratitude of Horus shall shine on you. My little Ackazarpses, how happy you are in having so royal a mistress.

   [His arm is round Ackazarpses' waist: she smiles at him.]

Queen: [rising]

Princes and gentlemen, let us drink to the future.

Priest of Horus: [starting suddenly]

Ah-h-h!

Queen:

Something has troubled you, holy companion of the gods?

Priest of Horus:

No, nothing. Sometimes the spirit of prophecy comes on me. It comes not often. It seemed to come then. I thought that one of the gods spoke to me clearly.

Queen:

What said he?

Priest of Horus:

I thought he said... speaking here [right ear] or just behind me... Drink not to the Future. But it was nothing.

Queen:

Will you drink then to the past?

Priest of Horus:

O no, Illustrious Lady, for we forget the past; your good wine has made us forget the past and its quarrels.

Ackazarpses:

Will you not drink to the present?

Priest of Horus:

Ah, the present! The present that places me by so lovely a lady. I drink to the present.

Queen: [to the others]

And we, we will drink to the future, and to forgetting--to the forgetting of our enemies.

[All drink; good temper comes on all. The banquet begins "to go well."]

Queen:

Ackazarpses, they are all merry now.

Ackazarpses:

They are all merry.

Queen:

They are telling Ethiopian tales.
1st Duke of Ethiopia:

...for when Winter comes the pigmies at once put themselves in readiness for war and having chosen a place for battle wait there for some days, so that the cranes when they arrive find their enemy already arrayed. And at first they preen themselves and do not give battle, but when they are fully rested after their great journey they attack the pigmies with indescribably fury so that many are slain, but the pigmies...

Queen: [taking her by the wrist]

Ackazarpses! Come!

[The Queen rises.]

Zophernes:

Queen, you do not leave us?

Queen:

For a little while, Prince Zophernes.

Zophernes:

For what purpose?

Queen:

I go to pray to a very secret god.

Zophernes:

What is his name?

Queen:

His name is secret like his deeds.

> [She goes to door. Silence falls. All watch her. She and Ackazarpses slip out. For a moment silence. Then all draw their wide swords and lay them before them on the table.]

Zophernes:

To the door, slaves. Let no man enter.

1st Duke of Ethiopia:

She cannot mean to harm us!

   [A Slave comes back from door and abases himself. Loq.]

Slave:

The door is bolted.

Rhadamandaspes:

It is easily broken with our swords.

Zophernes:

No harm can come to us while we guard the entrances.
   [Meanwhile the Queen has gone up the stairs. She beats with a fan on the wall thrice. The great grating lifts outwards and upwards very slowly.]

Zophernes: [to the Two Dukes]

Quick, to the great hole.

Stand on each side of it with your swords.

   [They lift their swords over the hole.]

Slay whatever enters.

Queen:

   [on the step, kneeling, her two arms stretched upwards]

O holy Nile! Ancient Egyptian river! O blessed Nile!

When I was a little child I played beside you, picking mauve flowers. I threw you down the sweet Egyptian flowers. It is the little Queen that calls to you, Nile. The little Queen that cannot bear to have enemies.

Hear me, O Nile.

Men speak of other rivers. But I do not hearken to fools. There is only Nile. It is the little child that prays to you who used to pick mauve flowers.

Hear me, O Nile.

I have prepared a sacrifice to god. Men speak of other gods: there is only Nile. I have prepared a sacrifice of wine--the Lesbian wine from fairy Mitylene--to mingle with your waters till you are drunken and go singing to the sea from the Abyssinian hills.

O Nile, hear me.

Fruits also I have made ready, all the sweet juices of the earth; and the meat of beasts also.

Hear me, O Nile: for it is not the meat of beasts only. I have slaves for you and princes and a King. There has been no such sacrifice. Come down, O Nile, from the sunlight. O ancient Egyptian river!

The sacrifice is ready. O Nile, hear me.

Duke of Ethiopia:

No one comes.

Queen: [beats again with her fan]

Harlee, Harlee, let in the water upon the princes and gentlemen.

> [A green torrent descends from the great hole. Green gauzes rise from the floor; the torches hiss out. The temple is flooded. The water from under the doors rises up the steps, the torches hiss out one by one. The water, finding its own level, just touches the end of the Queen's skirt and stops. She withdraws the skirt with catlike haste from the water.]

Queen:

O Ackazarpses! Are all my enemies gone?

Ackazarpses:

Illustrious Lady, the Nile has taken them all.

Queen: [with intense devotion]

That holy river.

Ackazarpses:

Illustrious Lady, will you sleep to-night?

Queen:

Yes. I shall sleep sweetly.

 [curtain]

The Tents of the Arabs

Dramatis Personae

The King
Bel-Narb, Aoob (camel-drivers)
The Chamberlain
Zabra (a notable)
Eznarza (a gypsy of the desert)

Scene: Outside the gate of the city of Thalanna.

Time: Uncertain.

Act I

Bel-Narb:

By evening we shall be in the desert again.

Aoob:

Yes.

Bel-Narb:

Then no more city for us for many weeks.

Aoob:

Ah!

Bel-Narb:

We shall see the lights come out, looking back from the camel-track; that is the last we shall see of it.

Aoob:

We shall be in the desert then.

Bel-Narb:

The old angry desert.

Aoob:

How cunningly the Desert hides his wells. You would say he had an enmity with man. He does not welcome you as the cities do.

Bel-Narb:

He has an enmity. I hate the desert.

Aoob:

I think there is nothing in the world so beautiful as cities.

Bel-Narb:

Cities are beautiful things.

Aoob:

I think they are loveliest a little after dawn when night falls off from the houses. They draw it away from them slowly and let it fall like a cloak and stand quite naked in their beauty to shine in some broad river; and the light comes up and kisses them on the forehead. I think they are loveliest then. The voices of men and women begin to arise in the streets, scarce audible, one by one, till a slow loud murmur arises and all the voices are one. I often think the city speaks to me then: she says in that voice of hers, "Aoob, Aoob, who one of these days shall die, I am not earthly, I have been always, I shall not die."

Bel-Narb:

I do not think that cities are loveliest at dawn. We can see dawn in the desert any day. I think they are loveliest just when the sun is set and a dusk steals along the narrower streets, a kind of mystery in which we can see cloaked figures and yet not quite discern whose figures they be. And just when it would be dark, and out in the desert there would be nothing to see but a black horizon and a black sky on top of it, just then the swinging lanterns are lighted up and lights come out in windows one by one and all the colours of the raiments change. Then a woman perhaps will slip from a little door and go away up the street into the night, and a man perhaps will steal by with a dagger for some old quarrel's sake, and Skarmi will light up his house to sell brandy all night long, and men will sit on benches outside his door playing skabash by the glare of a small green lantern, while they light great bubbling pipes and smoke nargroob. O, it is all very good to watch. And I like to think as I smoke and see these things that somewhere, far away, the desert has put up a huge red cloud like a wing so that all the Arabs know that next day the Siroc will blow, the accursed breath of Eblis the father of Satan.

Aoob:

Yes, it is pleasant to think of the Siroc when one is safe in a city, but I do not like to think about it now, for before the day is out we will be taking pilgrims to Mecca, and who ever prophesied or knew by wit what the desert had in store? Going into the desert is like throwing bone after bone to a dog, some he will catch and some of them he will drop. He may catch our bones, or we may go by and come to gleaming Mecca. O-ho, I would I were a merchant with a little booth in a frequented street to sit all day and barter.

Bel-Narb:

Aye, it is easier to cheat some lord coming to buy silk and ornaments in a city than to cheat death in the desert. Oh, the desert, the desert, I love the beautiful cities and I hate the desert.

Aoob: [pointing off L]

Who is that?

Bel-Narb:

What? There by the desert's edge where the camels are?

Aoob:

Yes, who is it?

Bel-Narb:

He is staring across the desert the way that the camels go. They say that the King goes down to the edge of the desert and often stares across it. He stands there for a long time of an evening looking towards Mecca.

Aoob:

Of what use is it to the King to look towards Mecca? He cannot go to Mecca. He cannot go into the desert for one day. Messengers would run after him and cry his name and bring him back to the council-hall or to the chamber of judgments. If they could not find him their heads would be struck off and put high up upon some windy roof: the judges would point at them and say, "They see better there!"

Bel-Narb:

No, the King cannot go away into the desert. If God were to make me King I would go down to the edge of the desert once, and I would shake the sand out of my turban and out of my beard and then I would never look at the desert again. Greedy and parched old parent of thousands of devils! He might cover the wells with sand, and blow with his Siroc, year after year and century after century, and never earn one of my curses--if God made me King.

Aoob:

They say you are like the King.

Bel-Narb:

Yes, I am like the King. Because his father disguised himself as a camel-driver and came through our villages. I often say to myself, "God is just. And if I could disguise myself as the King and drive him out to be a camel-driver, that would please God for He is just."

Aoob:

If you did this God would say, "Look at Bel-Narb, whom I made to be a camel-driver and who has forgotten this." And then he would forget you, Bel-Narb.

Bel-Narb:

Who knows what God would say?

Aoob:

Who knows? His ways are wonderful.

Bel-Narb:

I would not do this thing, Aoob. I would not do it. It is only what I say to myself as I smoke, or at night out in the desert. I say to myself, "Bel-Narb is King in Thalanna." And then I say, "Chamberlain, bring Skarmi here with his brandy and his lanterns and boards to play skabash, and let all the town come and drink before the palace and magnify my name."

Pilgrims: [calling off L.]

Bel-Narb! Bel-Narb! Child of two dogs. Come and untether your camels. Come and start for holy Mecca.

Bel-Narb:

A curse on the desert.

Aoob:

The camels are rising. The caravan starts for Mecca. Farewell, beautiful city.

[Pilgrims' voices off: "Bel-Narb! Bel-Narb!"]

Bel-Narb:

I come, children of sin.

[Exeunt Bel-Narb and Aoob.]

[The King enters through the great door crowned. He sits upon the step.]

King:

A crown should not be worn upon the head. A sceptre should not be carried in Kings' hands. But a crown should be wrought into a golden chain, and a sceptre driven stake-wise into the ground so that a King may be chained to it by the ankle. Then he would know that he might not stray away into the beautiful desert and might never see the palm trees by the wells. O Thalanna, Thalanna, how I hate this city with its narrow, narrow ways, and evening after evening drunken men playing skabash in the scandalous gambling house of that old scoundrel Skarmi. O that I might marry the child of some unkingly house that generation to generation had never known a city, and that we might ride from here down the long track through the desert, always we two alone till we came to the tents of the Arabs. And the crown--some foolish, greedy man should be given it to his sorrow. And all this may not be, for a King is yet a King.

[Enter Chamberlain through door.]

Chamberlain:

Your Majesty!

King:

Well, my lord Chamberlain, have you more work for me to do?

Chamberlain:

Yes, there is much to do.

King:

I had hoped for freedom this evening, for the faces of the camels are towards Mecca, and I would see the caravans move off into the desert where I may not go.

Chamberlain:

There is very much for your Majesty to do. Iktra has revolted.

King:

Where is Iktra?

Chamberlain:

It is a little country tributary to your Majesty, beyond Zebdarlon, up among the hills.

King:

Almost, had it not been for this, almost I had asked you to let me go away among the camel-drivers to golden Mecca. I have done the work of a King now for five years and listened to my councilors, and all the while the desert called to me; he said, "Come to the tents of my children, to the tents of my children!" And all the while I dwelt among these walls.

Chamberlain:

If your majesty left the city now----

King:

I will not, we must raise an army to punish the men of Iktra.

Chamberlain:

Your Majesty will appoint the commanders by name. A tribe of your Majesty's fighting men must be summoned from Agrarva and another from Coloono, the jungle city, as well as one from Mirsk. This must be done by warrants sealed by your hand. Your Majesty's advisers await you in the council-hall.

King:

The sun is very low. Why have the caravans not started yet?

Chamberlain:

I do not know. And then your Majesty----

King: [laying his hand on the Chamberlain's arm]

Look, look! It is the shadows of the camels moving towards Mecca. How silently they slip over the ground, beautiful shadows. Soon they are out in the desert flat on the golden sands. And then the sun will set and they will be one with night.

Chamberlain:

If your Majesty has time for such things there are the camels themselves.

King:

No, no, I do not wish to watch the camels. They can never take me out to the beautiful desert to be free forever from cities. Here I must stay to do the work of a King. Only my dreams can go, and the shadows of the camels carry them, to find peace by the tents of the Arabs.

Chamberlain:

Will your Majesty now come to the council-hall?

King:

Yes, yes, I come.

   [Voices off: "Ho-Yo! *Ho-*Yay! ...*Ho-*Yo! *Ho-*Yay!"]

Now the whole caravan has started. Hark to the drivers of the baggage-camels. They will run behind them for the first ten miles, and tomorrow they will mount them. They will be out of sight of Thalanna then, and the desert will lie all round them with sunlight falling on its golden smiles. And a new look will come into their faces. I am sure that the desert whispers to them by night saying, "Be at peace, my children, at peace, my children."

[Meanwhile the Chamberlain has opened the door for the King and is waiting there bowing, with his hand resolutely on the opened door.]

Chamberlain:

Your Majesty will come to the council-hall?

King:

Yes, I will come. Had it not been for Iktra I might have gone away and lived in the golden desert for a year, and seen holy Mecca.

Chamberlain:

Perhaps your Majesty might have gone had it not been for Iktra.

King:

My curse upon Iktra! [He goes through the doorway.]

[As they stand in doorway enter Zabra R.]

Zabra:

Your Majesty.

King:

O-ho. More work for an unhappy King.

Zabra:

Iktra is pacified.

King:

Is pacified?

Zabra:

It happened suddenly. The men of Iktra met with a few of your Majesty's fighting men and an arrow chanced to kill the leader of the revolt, and therefore the mob fled away although they were many, and they have all cried for three hours, "Great is the King!"

King:

I will even yet see Mecca and the dreamed-of tents of the Arabs. I will go down now into the golden sands, I----

Chamberlain:

Your Majesty----

King:

In a few years I will return to you.

Chamberlain:

Your Majesty, it cannot be. We could not govern the people for more than a year. They would say, "The King is dead, the King----"

King:

Then I will return in a year. In one year only.

Chamberlain:

It is a long time, your Majesty.

King:

I will return at noon a year from to-day.

Chamberlain:

But, your Majesty, a princess is being sent for from Tharba.

King:

I thought one was coming from Karshish.

Chamberlain:

It has been thought more advisable that your Majesty should wed in Tharba. The passes across the mountains belong to the King of Tharba and he has great traffic with Sharan and the Isles.

King:

Let it be as you will.

Chamberlain:

But, your Majesty, the ambassadors start this week; the princess will be here in three months' time.

King:

Let her come in a year and a day.

Chamberlain:

Your Majesty!

King:

Farewell, I am in haste. I go to make ready for the desert. [Exit through door still speaking.] The olden, golden mother of happy men.

Chamberlain: [to Zabra]

One from whom God had not withheld all wisdom would not have given that message to our crazy young King.

Zabra:

But it must be known. Many things might happen if it were not known at once.

Chamberlain:

I knew it this morning. He is off to the desert now.

Zabra:

That is evil indeed; but we can lure him back.

Chamberlain:

Perhaps not for many days.

Zabra:

The King's favour is like gold.

Chamberlain:

It is like much gold. Who are the Arabs that the King's favour should be cast among them? The walls of their houses are canvas. Even the common snail has a finer wall to his house.

Zabra:

O, it is most evil. Alas that I told him this! We shall be poor men.

Chamberlain:

No one will give us gold for many days.

Zabra:

Yet you will govern Thalanna while he is away. You can increase the taxes of the merchants and the tribute of the men that till the fields.

Chamberlain:

They will only pay taxes and tribute to the King, who gives of his bounty to just and upright men when he is in Thalanna. But while he is away the surfeit of his wealth will go to unjust men and to men whose beards are unclean and who fear not God.

Zabra:

We shall indeed be poor.

Chamberlain:

A little gold perhaps from evil-doers for justice. Or a little money to decide the dispute of some righteous wealthy man; but no more till the King returns, whom God prosper.

Zabra:

God increase him. Will you yet try to detain him?

Chamberlain:

No. When he comes by with his retinue and escort I will walk beside his horse and tell him that a progress through the desert will well impress the Arabs with his splendour and turn their hearts towards him. And I will speak privily to some captain at the rear of the escort and he shall afterwards speak to the chief commander that he may lose the camel-track in a few days' time and take the King and his followers to wander in the desert and so return by chance to Thalanna again. And it may yet be well with us. We will wait here till they come by.

Zabra:

Will the chief commander do this thing certainly?

Chamberlain:

Yes, he will be one Thakbar, a poor man and a righteous.

Zabra:

But if he be not Thakbar but some greedy man who demands more gold than we would give to Thakbar?

Chamberlain:

Why, then we must give him even what he demands, and God will punish his greed.

Zabra:

He must come past us here.

Chamberlain:

Yes, he must come this way. He will summon the cavalry from the Saloia Samang.

Zabra:

It will be nearly dark before they can come.

Chamberlain:

No, he is in great haste. He will pass before sunset. He will make them mount at once.

Zabra: [looking off R.]

I do not see stir at the Saloia.

Chamberlain: [looking, too] No--no. I do not see. He will make a stir.

> [As they look a man comes through the doorway wearing a coarse brown cloak which falls over his forehead. Exit furtively L.]

What man is that? He has gone down to the camels.

Zabra:

He has given a piece of money to one of the camel-drivers.

Chamberlain:

See, he has mounted.

Zabra:

Can it have been the King!

> [Voice off L. "Ho-Yo! Ho-Yay!"]

Chamberlain:

It is only some camel-driver going into the desert. How glad his voice sounds.

Zabra:

The Siroc will swallow him.

Chamberlain:

What--if it were the King!

Zabra:

Why, if it were the King we should starve for a year.

[One year elapses between the first and second acts.]

Act II

[The same scene.]

[The King, wrapped in a camel-driver's cloak, sits by Eznarza, a gypsy of the desert.]

King:

Now I have known the desert and dwelt in the tents of the Arabs.

Eznarza:

There is no land like the desert and like the Arabs no people.

King:

It is all over and done; I return to the walls of my fathers.

Eznarza:

Time cannot put it away; I go back to the desert that nursed me.

King:

Did you think in those days on the sands, or among the tents in the mornings, that my year would ever end, and I be brought away by strength of my word to the prisoning of a palace?

Eznarza:

I knew that Time would do it, for my people have learned the way of him.

King:

Is it then Time that has mocked our futile prayers? Is he then greater than God that he has laughed at our praying?

Eznarza:

We may not say that he is greater than God. Yet we prayed that our own year might not pass away. God could not save it.

King:

Yes, yes. We prayed that prayer. All men would laugh at it.

Eznarza:

The prayer was not laughable. Only he that is lord of the years is obdurate. If a man prayed for life to a furious, merciless Sultan well might the Sultan's slaves laugh. Yet it is not laughable to pray for life.

King:

Yes, we are slaves of Time. To-morrow brings the princess who comes from Tharba. We must bow our heads.

Eznarza:

My people say that Time lives in the desert. He lies there in the sun.

King:

No, no, not in the desert. Nothing alters there.

Eznarza:

My people say that the desert is his country. He smites not his own country, my people say. But he overwhelms all other lands of the world.

King:

Yes, the desert is always the same, even the littlest rocks of it.

Eznarza:

They say that he loves the Sphinx and does not harm her. They say that he does not dare to harm the Sphinx. She has borne him many gods whom the infidels worship.

King:

Their father is more terrible than all the false gods.

Eznarza:

O, that he had but spared our little year.

King:

He destroys all things utterly.

Eznarza:

There is a little child of man that is mightier than he, and who saves the world from Time.

King:

Who is this little child that is mightier than Time? Is it Love that is mightier?

Eznarza:

No, not Love.

King:

If he conquers even Love then none are mightier.

Eznarza:

He scares Love away with weak white hairs and with wrinkles. Poor little Love, poor Love, Time scares him away.

King:

What is this child of man that can conquer Time and that is braver than Love?

Eznarza:

Even Memory.

King:

Yes. I will call to him when the wind is from the desert and the locusts are beaten against my obdurate walls. I will call to him more when I cannot see the desert and cannot hear the wind of it.

Eznarza:

He shall bring back our year to us that Time cannot destroy. Time cannot slaughter it if Memory says no. It is reprieved, though banished. We shall often see it though a little far off and all its hours and days shall dance to us and go by one by one and come back and dance again.

King:

Why, that is true. They shall come back to us. I had thought that they that work miracles whether in Heaven or Earth were unable to do one thing. I thought that they could not bring back days again when once they had fallen into the hands of Time.

Eznarza:

It is a trick that Memory can do. He comes up softly in the town or the desert, wherever a few men are, like the strange dark conjurors who sing to snakes, and he does his trick before them, and does it again and again.

King:

We will often make him bring the old days back when you are gone to your people and I am miserably wedded to the princess coming from Tharba.

Eznarza:

They will come with sand on their feet from the golden, beautiful desert; they will come with a long-gone sunset each one over his head. Their lips will laugh with the olden evening voices.

King:

It is nearly noon. It is nearly noon. It is nearly noon.

Eznarza:

Why, we part then.

King:

O, come into the city and be Queen there. I will send its princess back again to Tharba. You shall be Queen in Thalanna.

Eznarza:

I go now back to my people. You will wed the princess from Tharba on the morrow. You have said it. I have said it.

King:

O, that I had not given my word to return.

Eznarza:

A King's word is like a King's crown and a King's sceptre and a King's throne. It is in fact a foolish thing, like a city.

King:

I cannot break my word. But you can be Queen in Thalanna.

Eznarza:

Thalanna will not have a gypsy for a Queen.

King:

I will make Thalanna have her for a Queen.

Eznarza:

You cannot make a gypsy live for a year in a city.

King:

I knew of a gypsy that lived once in a city.

Eznarza:

Not such a gypsy as I... come back to the tents of the Arabs.

King:

I cannot. I gave my word.

Eznarza:

Kings have broken their words.

King:

Not such a King as I.

Eznarza:

We have only that little child of man whose name is Memory.

King:

Come. He shall bring back to us, before we part, one of those days that were banished.

Eznarza:

Let it be the first day. The day we met by the well when the camels came to El-Lolith.

King:

Our year lacked some few days. For my year began here. The camels were some days out.

Eznarza:

You were riding a little wide of the caravan, upon the side of the sunset. Your camel was swinging on with easy strides. But you were tired.

King:

You had come to the well for water. At first I could see your eyes, then the stars came out, and it grew dark and I only saw your shape, and there was a little light about your hair: I do not know if it was the light of the stars, I only knew that it shone.

Eznarza:

And then you spoke to me about the camels.

King:

Then I heard your voice. You did not say the things you would say now.

Eznarza:

Of course I did not.

King:

You did not say things in the same way even.

Eznarza:

How the hours come dancing back!

King:

No, no. Only their shadows. We went together then to Holy Mecca. We dwelt alone in tents in the golden desert. We heard the wild free day sing sings in his freedom, we heard the beautiful night wind. Nothing remains of our year but desolate shadows. Memory whips them and they will not dance.

   [Eznarza does not answer.]

We made our farewells where the desert was. The city shall not hear them.

   [Eznarza covers her face. The King rises softly and walks up the steps. Enter L. the Chamberlain and Zabra, only noticing each other.]

Chamberlain:

He will come. He will come.

Zabra:

But it is noon now. Our fatness has left us. Our enemies mock at us. If he do not come God has forgotten us and our friends will pity us!

   [Enter Bel-Narb and Aoob.]

Chamberlain:

If he is alive he will come.

Zabra:

I fear that it is past noon.

Chamberlain:

Then he is dead or robbers have waylaid him.

   [Chamberlain and Zabra put dust upon their heads.]

Bel-Narb: [To Aoob.]

God is just!

   [To Chamberlain and Zabra.]

I am the King!

   [The King's hand is on the door. When Bel-Narb says this he goes down the steps again and sits beside the gypsy. She raises her head from her hands and looks at him fixedly. He watches Bel-Narb, and the Chamberlain and Zabra. He partially covers his face Arab fashion.]

Chamberlain:

Are you indeed the King?

Bel-Narb:

I am the King.

Chamberlain:

Your Majesty has altered much since a year ago.

Bel-Narb:

Men alter in the desert. And alter much.

Aoob:

Indeed, your Excellency, he is the King. When the King went into the desert disguised I fed his camel. Indeed he is the King.

Zabra:

He is the King. I know the King when I see him.

Chamberlain:

You have seen the King seldom.

Zabra:

I have often seen the King.

Bel-Narb:

Yes, we have often met, often and often.

Chamberlain:

If some one could recognize your Majesty, some one besides this man who came with you, then we should all be certain.

Bel-Narb:

There is no need of it. I am the King.

   [The King rises and stretches out his hand palm downwards.]

King:

In holy Mecca, in green-roofed Mecca of the many gates, we knew him for the King.

Bel-Narb:

Yes, that is true. I saw this man in Mecca.

Chamberlain: [Bowing low.]

Pardon, your Majesty. The desert had altered you.

Zabra:

I knew your Majesty.

Aoob:

As well as I do.

Bel-Narb: [Pointing to the King.]

Let this man be rewarded suitably. Give him some post in the palace.

Chamberlain:

Yes, your Majesty.

King:

I am a camel-driver and we go back to our camels.

Chamberlain:

As you wish.

[Exeunt Bel-Narb, Aoob, Chamberlain and Zabra through door.]

Eznarza:

You have done wisely, wisely, and the reward of wisdom is happiness.

King:

They have their king now. But we will turn again to the tents of the Arabs.

Eznarza:

They are foolish people.

King:

They have found a foolish King.

Eznarza:

It is a foolish man that would choose to dwell among walls.

King:

Some are born kings, but this man has chosen to be one.

Eznarza:

Come, let us leave them.

King:

We will go back again.

Eznarza:

Come back to the tents of my people.

King:

We will dwell a little apart in a dear brown tent of our own.

Eznarza:

We shall hear the sand again, whispering low to the dawn wind.

King:

We shall hear the nomads stirring in their camps far off because it is dawn.

Eznarza:

The jackals will patter past us slipping back to the hills.

King:

When at evening the sun is set we shall weep for no day that is gone.

Eznarza:

I will raise up my head of a night time against the sky, and the old, old, unbought stars shall twinkle through my hair, and we shall not envy any of the diademmed queens of the world.

CURTAIN

A Night at an Inn

Dramatis Personae

A. E. Scott-Fortescue (the Toff, dilapidated gentleman)
William Jones (Bill)
Albert Thomas
Jacob Smith (Sniggers) (All Merchant Sailors.)
1st Priest of Klesh
2nd Priest of Klesh
3rd Priest of Klesh
Klesh

[The Curtain rises on a room in an inn.]

[Sniggers and Bill are talking. The Toff is reading a paper. Albert sits a little apart.]

Sniggers:

What's his idea, I wonder?

Bill:

I don't know.

Sniggers:

And how much longer will he keep us here?

Bill:

We've been here three days.

Sniggers:

And 'aven't seen a soul.

Bill:

And a pretty penny it cost us when he rented the pub.

Sniggers:

'Ow long did 'e rent the pub for?

Bill:

You never know with him.

Sniggers:

It's lonely enough.

Bill:

'Ow long did you rent the pub for, Toffy?

    [The Toff continues to read a sporting paper; he takes no notice of what is said.]

Sniggers:

'E's such a toff.

Bill:

Yet 'e's clever, no mistake.

Sniggers:

Those clever ones are the beggars to make a muddle. Their plans are clever enough, but they don't work, and then they make a mess of things much worse than you or me.

Bill:

Ah

Sniggers:

I don't like this place.

Bill:

Why not?

Sniggers:

I don't like the looks of it.

Bill:

He's keeping us here because those niggers can't find us. The three heathen priests what was looking for us so. But we want to go and sell our ruby soon.

Albert:

There's no sense in it.

Bill:

Why not, Albert?

Albert:

Because I gave those black devils the slip in Hull.

Bill:

You give 'em the slip, Albert?

Albert:

The slip, all three of them. The fellows with the gold spots on their foreheads. I had the ruby then, and I give them the slip in Hull.

Bill:

How did you do it, Albert?

Albert:

I had the ruby and they were following me....

Bill:

Who told them you had the ruby? You didn't show it?

Albert:

No.... But they kind of know.

Sniggers:

They kind of know, Albert?

Albert:

Yes, they know if you've got it. Well, they sort of mouched after me, and I tells a policeman and he says, O they were only three poor niggers and they wouldn't hurt me. Ugh! When I thought of what they did in Malta to poor old Jim.

Bill:

Yes, and to George in Bombay before we started.

Sniggers:

Ugh!

Bill:

Why didn't you give 'em in charge?

Albert:

What about the ruby, Bill?

Bill:

Ah!

Albert:

Well, I did better than that. I walks up and down through Hull. I walks slow enough. And then I turns a corner and I runs. I never sees a corner but I turns it. But sometimes I let a corner pass just to fool them. I twists about like a hare. Then I sits down and waits. No priests.

Sniggers:

What?

Albert:

No heathen black devils with gold spots on their face. I give 'em the slip.

Bill:

Well done, Albert.

Sniggers: [after a sigh of content]

Why didn't you tell us?

Albert:

'Cause 'e won't let you speak. 'E's got 'is plans and 'e thinks we're silly folk. Things must be done 'is way. And all the time I've give 'em the slip. Might 'ave 'ad one of them crooked knives in him before now but for me who give 'em the slip in Hull.

Bill:

Well done, Albert.

Sniggers:

Do you hear that, Toffy? Albert has give 'em the slip.

The Toff:

Yes, I hear.

Sniggers:

Well, what do you say to that?

The Toff:

O... Well done, Albert.

Albert:

And what a' you going to do?

The Toff:

Going to wait.

Albert:

Don't seem to know what 'e's waiting for.

Sniggers:

It's a nasty place.

Albert:

It's getting silly, Bill. Our money's gone and we want to sell the ruby. Let's get on to a town.

Bill:

But 'e won't come.

Albert:

Then we'll leave him.

Sniggers:

We'll be all right if we keep away from Hull.

Albert:

We'll go to London.

Bill:

But 'e must 'ave 'is share.

Sniggers:

All right. Only let's go. [to the Toff] We're going, do you hear? Give us the ruby.

The Toff:

Certainly.

>[He gives them a ruby from his waistcoat pocket: it is the size of a small hen's egg.]

>[He goes on reading his paper.]

Albert:

Come on, Sniggers.

>[Exeunt Albert and Sniggers.]

Bill:

Good-bye, old man. We'll give you your fair share, but there's nothing to do here, no girls, no halls, and we must sell the ruby.

The Toff:

I'm not a fool, Bill.

Bill:

No, no, of course not. Of course you ain't, and you've helped us a lot. Good-bye. You'll say good-bye?

The Toff:

Oh, yes. Good-bye.

   [Still reads paper. Exit Bill.]

   [The Toff puts a revolver on the table beside him and goes on with his paper.]

Sniggers: [Out of breath.]

We've come back, Toffy.

The Toff:

So you have.

Albert:

Toffy--How did they get here?

The Toff:

They walked, of course.

Albert:

But it's eighty miles.

Sniggers:

Did you know they were here, Toffy?

The Toff:

Expected them about now.

Albert:

Eighty miles.

Bill:

Toffy, old man--what are we to do?

The Toff:

Ask Albert.

Bill:

If they can do things like this there's no one can save us but you, Toffy--I always knew you were a clever one. We won't be fools any more. We'll obey you, Toffy.

The Toff:

You're brave enough and strong enough. There isn't many that would steal a ruby eye out of an idol's head, and such an idol as that was to look at, and on such a night. You're brave enough, Bill. But you're all three of you fools. Jim would have none of my plans and where's Jim? And George. What did they do to him?

Sniggers:

Don't, Toffy!

The Toff:

Well, then, your strength is no use to you. You want cleverness; or they'll have you the way that they had George and Jim.

All:

Ugh!

The Toff:

Those black priests would follow you round the world in circles, year after year, till they got the idol's eye. And if we died with it they'd follow our grandchildren. That fool thinks he can escape men like that by running round three streets in the town of Hull.

Albert:

God's truth, you *'aven't escaped them, because they're* 'ere.

The Toff:

So I supposed.

Albert:

You supposed?

The Toff:

Yes, I believe there's no announcement in the Society papers. But I took this country seat especially to receive them. There's plenty of room if you dig; it is pleasantly situated and what is most important it is in a very quiet neighbourhood. So I am at home to them this afternoon.

Bill:

Well, you're a deep one.

The Toff:

And remember you've only my wits between you and death, and don't put your futile plans against those of an educated gentleman.

Albert:

If you're a gentleman, why don't you go about among gentlemen instead of the likes of us?

The Toff:

Because I was too clever for them as I am too clever for you.

Albert:

Too clever for them?

The Toff:

I never lost a game of cards in my life.

Bill:

You never lost a game?

The Toff:

Not when there was money on it.

Bill:

Well, well.

The Toff:

Have a game of poker?

All:

No, thanks.

The Toff:

Then do as you're told.

Bill:

All right, Toffy.

Sniggers:

I saw something just then. Hadn't we better draw the curtains?

The Toff:

No.

Sniggers:

What?

The Toff:

Don't draw the curtains.

Sniggers:

O all right.

Bill:

But Toffy, they can see us. One doesn't let the enemy do that. I don't see why....

The Toff:

No, of course you don't.

Bill:

O all right, Toffy.

[All begin to pull out revolvers.]

The Toff: [putting his own away]

No revolvers, please.

Albert:

Why not?

The Toff:

Because I don't want any noise at my party. We might get guests that hadn't been invited. Knives are a different matter.

[All draw knives. The Toff signs to them not to draw them yet. Toffy has already taken back his ruby.]

Bill:

I think they're coming, Toffy.

The Toff:

Not yet.

Albert:

When will they come?

The Toff:

When I am quite ready to receive them. Not before.

Sniggers:

I should like to get this over.

The Toff:

Should you? Then we'll have them now.

Sniggers:

Now?

The Toff:

Yes. Listen to me. You shall do as you see me do. You will all pretend to go out. I'll show you how. I've got the ruby. When they see me alone they will come for their idol's eye.

Bill:

How can they tell like this which one of us has it?

The Toff:

I confess I don't know, but they seem to.

Sniggers:

What will you do when they come in?

The Toff:

I shall do nothing.

Sniggers:

What?

The Toff:

They will creep up behind me. Then my friends, Sniggers and Bill and Albert, who gave them the slip, will do what they can.

Bill:

All right, Toffy. Trust us.

The Toff:

If you're a little slow you will see enacted the cheerful spectacle that accompanied the demise of Jim.

Sniggers:

Don't, Toffy. We'll be there all right.

The Toff:

Very well. Now watch me.

> [He goes past the windows to the inner door R.; he opens it inwards. Then under cover of the open door he slips down on his knee and closes it, remaining on the inside, appearing to have gone out. He signs to the others who understand. Then he appears to re-enter in the same manner.]

Now, I shall sit with my back to the door. You go out one by one so far as our friends can make out. Crouch very low to be on the safe side. They mustn't see you through the window.

[Bill makes his sham exit.]

The Toff:

Remember, no revolvers. The police are, I believe, proverbially inquisitive.

[The other two follow Bill. All three are now crouching inside the door R. The Toff puts the ruby beside him on the table. He lights a cigarette.]

[The door in back opens so slowly that you can hardly say at what moment it began. The Toff picks up his paper.]

[A Native of India wriggles along the floor ever so slowly, seeking cover from chairs. He moves L. where the Toff is. The three sailors are R. Sniggers and Albert lean forward. Bill's arm keeps them back. An armchair had better conceal them from the Indian. The black Priest nears the Toff.]

[Bill watches to see if any more are coming. Then he leaps forward alone (he has taken his boots off) and knifes the Priest.]

[The Priest tries to shout but Bill's left hand is over his mouth.]

[The Toff continues to read his sporting paper. He never looks round.]

Bill: [sotto voce]

There's only one, Toffy. What shall we do?

The Toff: [without turning his head]

Only one?

Bill:

Yes.

The Toff:

Wait a moment. Let me think.

   [Still apparently absorbed in his paper.]

Ah, yes. You go back, Bill. We must attract another guest. Now are you ready?

Bill:

Yes.

The Toff:

All right. You shall now see my demise at my Yorkshire residence. You must receive guests for me.

   [He leaps up in full view of the window, flings up both arms and falls on to the floor near the dead Priest.]

Now be ready.

[His eyes close.]

[There is a long pause. Again the door opens, very very slowly. Another Priest creeps in. He has three golden spots upon his forehead. He looks round, then he creeps up to his companion and turns him over and looks inside each of his clenched hands. Then he looks at the recumbent Toff. Then he creeps towards him. Bill slips after him and knifes him like the other with his left hand over his mouth.]

Bill: [sotto voce]

We've only got two, Toffy.

The Toff:

Still another.

Bill:

What'll we do?

The Toff: [sitting up]

Hum.

Bill:

This is the best way, much.

The Toff:

Out of the question. Never play the same game twice.

Bill:

Why not, Toffy?

The Toff:

Doesn't work if you do.

Bill:

Well?

The Toff:

I have it, Albert. You will now walk into the room. I showed you how to do it.

Albert:

Yes.

The Toff:

Just run over here and have a fight at this window with these two men.

Albert:

But they're----

The Toff:

Yes, they're dead, my perspicuous Albert. But Bill and I are going to resuscitate them.----. Come on.

[Bill picks up a body under the arms.]

That's right, Bill. [Does the same.] Come and help us, Sniggers----
[Sniggers comes] Keep low, keep low. Wave their arms about, Sniggers. Don't show yourself. Now, Albert, over you go. Our Albert is slain. Back you get, Bill. Back, Sniggers. Still, Albert. Mustn't move when he comes. Not a muscle.

[A Face appears at the window and stays for some time. Then the door opens and looking craftily round the third Priest enters. He looks at his companions' bodies and turns round. He suspects something. He takes up one of the knives and with a knife in each hand he puts his back to the wall. He looks to the left and right.]

The Toff:

Come on, Bill.

[The Priest rushes to the door. The Toff knifes the last Priest from behind.]

The Toff:

A good day's work, my friends.

Bill:

Well done, Toffy. Oh, you are a deep one.

Albert:

A deep one if ever there was one.

Sniggers:

There ain't any more, Bill, are there?

The Toff:

No more in the world, my friend.

Bill:

Aye, that's all there are. There were only three in the temple. Three priests and their beastly idol.

Albert:

What is it worth, Toffy? Is it worth a thousand pounds?

The Toff:

It's worth all they've got in the shop. Worth just whatever we like to ask for it.

Albert:

Then we're millionaires, now.

The Toff:

Yes, and what is more important, we no longer have any heirs.

Bill:

We'll have to sell it now.

Albert:

That won't be easy. It's a pity it isn't small and we had half a dozen. Hadn't the idol any other on him?

Bill:

No, he was green jade all over and only had this one eye. He had it in the middle of his forehead, and was a long sight uglier than anything else in the world.

Sniggers:

I'm sure we ought all to be very grateful to Toffy.

Bill:

And indeed we ought.

Albert:

If it hadn't 'ave been for him----

Bill:

Yes, if it hadn't 'a' been for old Toffy....

Sniggers:

He's a deep one.

The Toff:

Well, you see, I just have a knack of foreseeing things.

Sniggers:

I should think you did.

Bill:

Why, I don't suppose anything happens that our Toff doesn't foresee. Does it, Toffy?

The Toff:

Well, I don't think it does, Bill. I don't think it often does.

Bill:

Life is no more than just a game of cards to our old Toff.

The Toff:

Well, we've taken these fellows' trick.

Sniggers: [going to the window]

It wouldn't do for any one to see them.

The Toff:

O nobody will come this way. We're all alone on a moor.

Bill:

Where will we put them?

The Toff:

Bury them in the cellar, but there's no hurry.

Bill:

And what then, Toffy?

The Toff:

Why, then we'll go to London and upset the ruby business. We'll have really come through this job very nicely.

Bill:

I think the first thing we ought to do is give a little supper to old Toffy. We'll bury these fellows to-night.

Albert:

Yes, let's.

Sniggers:

The very thing.

Bill:

And we'll all drink his health.

Albert:

Good old Toffy.

Sniggers:

He ought to have been a general or a premier.

   [They get bottles from cupboard, etc.]

The Toff:

Well, we've earned our bit of a supper.

   [They sit down.]

Bill: [Glass in hand.]

Here's to old Toffy who guessed everything.

Albert and Sniggers:

Good old Toffy.

Bill:

Toffy who saved our lives and made our fortunes.

Albert and Sniggers:

Hear. Hear.

The Toff:

And here's to Bill who saved me twice to-night.

Bill:

Couldn't have done it but for your cleverness, Toffy.

Sniggers:

Hear, hear. Hear, hear.

Albert:

He foresees everything.

Bill:

A speech, Toffy. A speech from our general.

All:

Yes, a speech.

Sniggers:

A speech.

The Toff:

Well, get me some water. This whiskey's too much for my head, and I must keep it clear till our friends are safe in the cellar.

Bill:

Water. Yes, of course. Get him some water, Sniggers.

Sniggers:

We don't use water here. Where shall I get it?

Bill:

Outside in the garden.

  [Exit Sniggers.]

Albert:

Here's to fortune. [They all drink.]

Bill:

Here's to Albert Thomas, Esquire. [He drinks.]

The Toff:

Albert Thomas, Esquire. [He drinks.]

Albert:

And William Jones Esquire.

The Toff:

Albert Jones, Esquire. [The Toff and Albert drink.]

[Re-enter Sniggers terrified.]

The Toff:

Hullo, here's Jacob Smith Esquire, J.P., alias Sniggers, back again.

Sniggers:

Toffy, I've been thinking about my share in that ruby. I don't want it, Toffy, I don't want it.

The Toff:

Nonsense, Sniggers, nonsense.

Sniggers:

You shall have it, Toffy, you shall have it yourself, only say Sniggers has no share in this 'ere ruby. Say it, Toffy, say it.

Bill:

Want to turn informer, Sniggers?

Sniggers:

No, no. Only I don't want the ruby, Toffy....

The Toff:

No more nonsense, Sniggers, we're all in together in this, if one hangs we all hang; but they won't outwit me. Besides, it's not a hanging affair, they had their knives.

Sniggers:

Toffy, Toffy, I've always treated you fair, Toffy. I was always one to say, Give Toffy a chance. Take back my share, Toffy.

The Toff:

What's the matter? What are you driving at?

Sniggers:

Take it back, Toffy.

The Toff:

Answer me; what are you up to?

Sniggers:

I don't want my share any more.

Bill:

Have you seen the police?

   [Albert pulls out his knife.]

The Toff:

No, no knives, Albert.

Albert:

What then?

The Toff:

The honest truth in open court, barring the ruby. We were attacked.

Sniggers:

There's no police.

The Toff:

Well, then, what's the matter?

Bill:

Out with it.

Sniggers:

I swear to God...

Albert:

Well?

The Toff:

Don't interrupt.

Sniggers:

I swear I saw something what I didn't like.

The Toff:

What you didn't like?

Sniggers: [In tears.]

O Toffy, Toffy, take it back. Take my share. Say you take it.

The Toff:

What has he seen?

   [Dead silence only broken by Sniggers' sobs. Then stony steps are heard.]

   [Enter a hideous Idol. It is blind and gropes its way. It gropes its way to the ruby and picks it up and screws it into a socket in the forehead.]

   [Sniggers still weeps softly; the rest stare in horror. The Idol steps out, not groping. Its steps move off then stops.]

The Toff:

O great heavens!

Albert: [In a childish, plaintive voice.]

What is it, Toffy?

Bill:

Albert, it is that obscene idol [in a whisper] come from India.

Albert:

It is gone.

Bill:

It has taken its eye.

Sniggers:

We are saved.

Off, a Voice: [With outlandish accent.]

Meestaire William Jones, Able Seaman.

> [The Toff has never spoken, never moved. He only gazes stupidly in horror.]

Bill:

Albert, Albert, what is this?

> [He rises and walks out. One moan is heard. Sniggers goes to window. He falls back sickly.]

Albert: [In a whisper.]

What has happened?

Sniggers:

I have seen it. I have seen it. O I have seen it. [He returns to table.]

The Toff: [Laying his hand very gently on Sniggers' arm, speaking softly and winningly.]

What was it, Sniggers?

Sniggers:

I have seen it.

Albert:

What?

Sniggers:

O.

Voice:

Meestaire Albert Thomas, Able Seaman.

Albert:

Must I go, Toffy? Toffy, must I go?

Sniggers: [Clutching him.]

Don't move.

Albert: [Going.]

Toffy, Toffy. [Exit.]

Voice:

Meestaire Jacob Smith, Able Seaman.

Sniggers:

I can't go, Toffy. I can't go. I can't do it.

   [He goes.]

Voice:

Meestaire Arnold Everett Scott-Fortescue, late Esquire, Able Seaman.

The Toff:

I did not foresee it. [Exit.]

CURTAIN.

www.bookjungle.com *email: sales@bookjungle.com fax: 630-214-0564 mail: Book Jungle PO Box 2226 Champaign, IL 61825*

The Codes Of Hammurabi And Moses
W. W. Davies

QTY

The discovery of the Hammurabi Code is one of the greatest achievements of archaeology, and is of paramount interest, not only to the student of the Bible, but also to all those interested in ancient history...

Religion **ISBN:** *1-59462-338-4* **Pages:** 132 *MSRP $12.95*

The Theory of Moral Sentiments
Adam Smith

QTY

This work from 1749. contains original theories of conscience amd moral judgment and it is the foundation for systemof morals.

Philosophy **ISBN:** *1-59462-777-0* **Pages:** 536 *MSRP $19.95*

Jessica's First Prayer
Hesba Stretton

QTY

In a screened and secluded corner of one of the many railway-bridges which span the streets of London there could be seen a few years ago, from five o'clock every morning until half past eight, a tidily set-out coffee-stall, consisting of a trestle and board, upon which stood two large tin cans, with a small fire of charcoal burning under each so as to keep the coffee boiling during the early hours of the morning when the work-people were thronging into the city on their way to their daily toil...

Childrens **ISBN:** *1-59462-373-2* **Pages:** 84 *MSRP $9.95*

My Life and Work
Henry Ford

QTY

Henry Ford revolutionized the world with his implementation of mass production for the Model T automobile. Gain valuable business insight into his life and work with his own auto-biography... "We have only started on our development of our country we have not as yet, with all our talk of wonderful progress, done more than scratch the surface. The progress has been wonderful enough but..."

Biographies/ **ISBN:** *1-59462-198-5* **Pages:** 300 *MSRP $21.95*

www.bookjungle.com *email: sales@bookjungle.com fax: 630-214-0564 mail: Book Jungle PO Box 2226 Champaign, IL 61825*

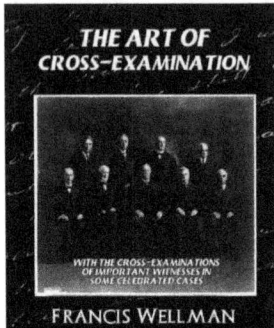

The Art of Cross-Examination
Francis Wellman

I presume it is the experience of every author, after his first book is published upon an important subject, to be almost overwhelmed with a wealth of ideas and illustrations which could readily have been included in his book, and which to his own mind, at least, seem to make a second edition inevitable. Such certainly was the case with me; and when the first edition had reached its sixth impression in five months, I rejoiced to learn that it seemed to my publishers that the book had met with a sufficiently favorable reception to justify a second and considerably enlarged edition. ..

Reference   ISBN: *1-59462-647-2*   Pages:412 MSRP *$19.95*

On the Duty of Civil Disobedience
Henry David Thoreau

Thoreau wrote his famous essay, On the Duty of Civil Disobedience, as a protest against an unjust but popular war and the immoral but popular institution of slave-owning. He did more than write—he declined to pay his taxes, and was hauled off to gaol in consequence. Who can say how much this refusal of his hastened the end of the war and of slavery ?

Law   ISBN: *1-59462-747-9*   Pages:48 MSRP *$7.45*

Dream Psychology Psychoanalysis for Beginners
Sigmund Freud

Sigmund Freud, born Sigismund Schlomo Freud (May 6, 1856 - September 23, 1939), was a Jewish-Austrian neurologist and psychiatrist who co-founded the psychoanalytic school of psychology. Freud is best known for his theories of the unconscious mind, especially involving the mechanism of repression; his redefinition of sexual desire as mobile and directed towards a wide variety of objects; and his therapeutic techniques, especially his understanding of transference in the therapeutic relationship and the presumed value of dreams as sources of insight into unconscious desires.

Psychology   ISBN: *1-59462-905-6*   Pages:196 MSRP *$15.45*

The Miracle of Right Thought
Orison Swett Marden

Believe with all of your heart that you will do what you were made to do. When the mind has once formed the habit of holding cheerful, happy, prosperous pictures, it will not be easy to form the opposite habit. It does not matter how improbable or how far away this realization may see, or how dark the prospects may be, if we visualize them as best we can, as vividly as possible, hold tenaciously to them and vigorously struggle to attain them, they will gradually become actualized, realized in the life. But a desire, a longing without endeavor, a yearning abandoned or held indifferently will vanish without realization.

Self Help   ISBN: *1-59462-644-8*   Pages:360 MSRP *$25.45*

www.bookjungle.com email: sales@bookjungle.com fax: 630-214-0564 mail: Book Jungle PO Box 2226 Champaign, IL 61825

QTY

	Title	ISBN	Price
☐	**The Rosicrucian Cosmo-Conception Mystic Christianity** by *Max Heindel*	1-59462-188-8	$38.95

The Rosicrucian Cosmo-conception is not dogmatic, neither does it appeal to any other authority than the reason of the student. It is: not controversial, but is: sent forth in the, hope that it may help to clear...
New Age/Religion Pages 646

☐ **Abandonment To Divine Providence** by *Jean-Pierre de Caussade* ISBN: 1-59462-228-0 $25.95
"The Rev. Jean Pierre de Caussade was one of the most remarkable spiritual writers of the Society of Jesus in France in the 18th Century. His death took place at Toulouse in 1751. His works have gone through many editions and have been republished...
Inspirational/Religion Pages 400

☐ **Mental Chemistry** by *Charles Haanel* ISBN: 1-59462-192-6 $23.95
Mental Chemistry allows the change of material conditions by combining and appropriately utilizing the power of the mind. Much like applied chemistry creates something new and unique out of careful combinations of chemicals the mastery of mental chemistry...
New Age Pages 354

☐ **The Letters of Robert Browning and Elizabeth Barret Barrett 1845-1846 vol II** ISBN: 1-59462-193-4 $35.95
by *Robert Browning* and *Elizabeth Barrett*
Biographies Pages 596

☐ **Gleanings In Genesis (volume I)** by *Arthur W. Pink* ISBN: 1-59462-130-6 $27.45
Appropriately has Genesis been termed "the seed plot of the Bible" for in it we have, in germ form, almost all of the great doctrines which are afterwards fully developed in the books of Scripture which follow...
Religion/Inspirational Pages 420

☐ **The Master Key** by *L. W. de Laurence* ISBN: 1-59462-001-6 $30.95
In no branch of human knowledge has there been a more lively increase of the spirit of research during the past few years than in the study of Psychology, Concentration and Mental Discipline. The requests for authentic lessons in Thought Control, Mental Discipline and...
New Age/Business Pages 422

☐ **The Lesser Key Of Solomon Goetia** by *L. W. de Laurence* ISBN: 1-59462-092-X $9.95
This translation of the first book of the "Lernegton" which is now for the first time made accessible to students of Talismanic Magic was done, after careful collation and edition, from numerous Ancient Manuscripts in Hebrew, Latin, and French...
New Age/Occult Pages 92

☐ **Rubaiyat Of Omar Khayyam** by *Edward Fitzgerald* ISBN:1-59462-332-5 $13.95
Edward Fitzgerald, whom the world has already learned, in spite of his own efforts to remain within the shadow of anonymity, to look upon as one of the rarest poets of the century, was born at Bredfield, in Suffolk, on the 31st of March, 1809. He was the third son of John Purcell...
Music Pages 172

☐ **Ancient Law** by *Henry Maine* ISBN: 1-59462-128-4 $29.95
The chief object of the following pages is to indicate some of the earliest ideas of mankind, as they are reflected in Ancient Law, and to point out the relation of those ideas to modern thought.
Religion/History Pages 452

☐ **Far-Away Stories** by *William J. Locke* ISBN: 1-59462-129-2 $19.45
"Good wine needs no bush, but a collection of mixed vintages does. And this book is just such a collection. Some of the stories I do not want to remain buried for ever in the museum files of dead magazine-numbers an author's not unpardonable vanity..."
Fiction Pages 272

☐ **Life of David Crockett** by *David Crockett* ISBN: 1-59462-250-7 $27.45
"Colonel David Crockett was one of the most remarkable men of the times in which he lived. Born in humble life, but gifted with a strong will, an indomitable courage, and unremitting perseverance...
Biographies/New Age Pages 424

☐ **Lip-Reading** by *Edward Nitchie* ISBN: 1-59462-206-X $25.95
Edward B. Nitchie, founder of the New York School for the Hard of Hearing, now the Nitchie School of Lip-Reading, Inc, wrote "LIP-READING Principles and Practice". The development and perfecting of this meritorious work on lip-reading was an undertaking...
How-to Pages 400

☐ **A Handbook of Suggestive Therapeutics, Applied Hypnotism, Psychic Science** ISBN: 1-59462-214-0 $24.95
by *Henry Munro*
Health/New Age/Health/Self-help Pages 376

☐ **A Doll's House: and Two Other Plays** by *Henrik Ibsen* ISBN: 1-59462-112-8 $19.95
Henrik Ibsen created this classic when in revolutionary 1848 Rome. Introducing some striking concepts in playwriting for the realist genre, this play has been studied the world over.
Fiction/Classics/Plays 308

☐ **The Light of Asia** by *sir Edwin Arnold* ISBN: 1-59462-204-3 $13.95
In this poetic masterpiece, Edwin Arnold describes the life and teachings of Buddha. The man who was to become known as Buddha to the world was born as Prince Gautama of India but he rejected the worldly riches and abandoned the reigns of power when...
Religion/History/Biographies Pages 170

☐ **The Complete Works of Guy de Maupassant** by *Guy de Maupassant* ISBN: 1-59462-157-8 $16.95
"For days and days, nights and nights, I had dreamed of that first kiss which was to consecrate our engagement, and I knew not on what spot I should put my lips..."
Fiction/Classics Pages 240

☐ **The Art of Cross-Examination** by *Francis L. Wellman* ISBN: 1-59462-309-0 $26.95
Written by a renowned trial lawyer, Wellman imparts his experience and uses case studies to explain how to use psychology to extract desired information through questioning.
How-to/Science/Reference Pages 408

☐ **Answered or Unanswered?** by *Louisa Vaughan* ISBN: 1-59462-248-5 $10.95
Miracles of Faith in China
Religion Pages 112

☐ **The Edinburgh Lectures on Mental Science (1909)** by *Thomas* ISBN: 1-59462-008-3 $11.95
This book contains the substance of a course of lectures recently given by the writer in the Queen Street Hall, Edinburgh. Its purpose is to indicate the Natural Principles governing the relation between Mental Action and Material Conditions...
New Age/Psychology Pages 148

☐ **Ayesha** by *H. Rider Haggard* ISBN: 1-59462-301-5 $24.95
Verily and indeed it is the unexpected that happens! Probably if there was one person upon the earth from whom the Editor of this, and of a certain previous history, did not expect to hear again...
Classics Pages 380

☐ **Ayala's Angel** by *Anthony Trollope* ISBN: 1-59462-352-X $29.95
The two girls were both pretty, but Lucy who was twenty-one who supposed to be simple and comparatively unattractive, whereas Ayala was credited, as her Bombwhat romantic name might show, with poetic charm and a taste for romance. Ayala when her father died was nineteen...
Fiction Pages 484

☐ **The American Commonwealth** by *James Bryce* ISBN: 1-59462-286-8 $34.45
An interpretation of American democratic political theory. It examines political mechanics and society from the perspective of Scotsman James Bryce
Politics Pages 572

☐ **Stories of the Pilgrims** by *Margaret P. Pumphrey* ISBN: 1-59462-116-0 $17.95
This book explores pilgrims religious oppression in England as well as their escape to Holland and eventual crossing to America on the Mayflower, and their early days in New England...
History Pages 268

www.bookjungle.com email: sales@bookjungle.com fax: 630-214-0564 mail: Book Jungle PO Box 2226 Champaign, IL 61825

QTY

The Fasting Cure *by Sinclair Upton* ISBN: *1-59462-222-1* **$13.95**
In the Cosmopolitan Magazine for May, 1910, and in the Contemporary Review (London) for April, 1910, I published an article dealing with my experiences in fasting. I have written a great many magazine articles, but never one which attracted so much attention... *New Age/Self Help/Health Pages 164*

Hebrew Astrology *by Sepharial* ISBN: *1-59462-308-2* **$13.45**
In these days of advanced thinking it is a matter of common observation that we have left many of the old landmarks behind and that we are now pressing forward to greater heights and to a wider horizon than that which represented the mind-content of our progenitors... *Astrology Pages 144*

Thought Vibration or The Law of Attraction in the Thought World ISBN: *1-59462-127-6* **$12.95**
by William Walker Atkinson *Psychology/Religion Pages 144*

Optimism *by Helen Keller* ISBN: *1-59462-108-X* **$15.95**
Helen Keller was blind, deaf, and mute since 19 months old, yet famously learned how to overcome these handicaps, communicate with the world, and spread her lectures promoting optimism. An inspiring read for everyone... *Biographies/Inspirational Pages 84*

Sara Crewe *by Frances Burnett* ISBN: *1-59462-360-0* **$9.45**
In the first place, Miss Minchin lived in London. Her home was a large, dull, tall one, in a large, dull square, where all the houses were alike, and all the sparrows were alike, and where all the door-knockers made the same heavy sound... *Childrens/Classic Pages 88*

The Autobiography of Benjamin Franklin *by Benjamin Franklin* ISBN: *1-59462-135-7* **$24.95**
The Autobiography of Benjamin Franklin has probably been more extensively read than any other American historical work, and no other book of its kind has had such ups and downs of fortune. Franklin lived for many years in England, where he was agent... *Biographies/History Pages 332*

Name	
Email	
Telephone	
Address	
City, State ZIP	

☐ Credit Card   ☐ Check / Money Order

Credit Card Number	
Expiration Date	
Signature	

Please Mail to: Book Jungle
PO Box 2226
Champaign, IL 61825
or Fax to: 630-214-0564

ORDERING INFORMATION

web: *www.bookjungle.com*
email: *sales@bookjungle.com*
fax: *630-214-0564*
mail: *Book Jungle PO Box 2226 Champaign, IL 61825*
or PayPal *to sales@bookjungle.com*

Please contact us for bulk discounts

DIRECT-ORDER TERMS

20% Discount if You Order Two or More Books
Free Domestic Shipping!
Accepted: Master Card, Visa, Discover, American Express

www.ingramcontent.com/pod-product-compliance
Lightning Source LLC
Chambersburg PA
CBHW081836170426
43199CB00017B/2748